HEALING FEELINGS

Release emotional pain
Change your past & future
Connect to your True Self

Geri O'Neill

To my dear Friend Ann,
With love,
Geri O'Neill

ISBN-10: 1512138630
ISBN-13: 978-1512138634

For my husband Ron
With deepest gratitude for his
Unwavering love, support and encouragement

CONTENTS

INTRODUCTION   7

This above all: to thine own self be true,
And it must follow, as the night the day,
Thou canst not then be false to any man.
William Shakespeare

CHAPTER 1   WHO ARE YOU?   9

All the world's a stage,
And all the men and women merely players;
They have their exits and their entrances,
And one man in his time plays many parts...
William Shakespeare

CHAPTER 2   FALSE SELF vs. TRUE SELF   14

God has given you one face, and you make yourself another.
William Shakespeare

CHAPTER 3   ENERGY PRESSES   18

Unexpressed emotions will never die.
They are buried alive and
will come forth later in uglier ways.
Sigmund Freud

CHAPTER 4   THE ANGRY CHILD WITHIN   23

Anger is an acid that can do more harm to the vessel in
which it is stored than to anything on which it is poured.
Mark Twain

CHAPTER 5   WEAVING PATTERNS   27

Your visions will become clear only when you can
look into your own heart.
Who looks outside, dreams; who looks inside, awakes.
C.G. Jung

CHAPTER 6   THE PAST IS PRESENT   31

The human body is the best picture of the human soul.
Ludwig Wittgenstein

CHAPTER 7 PASSION & ADDICTION   34

*If a person is to get the meaning of life he must learn to
like the facts about himself -- ugly as they may seem to
his sentimental vanity -- before he can learn the truth
behind the facts.*
Eugene O'Neill

CHAPTER 8 THOUGHT – EMOTION – ACTION 39

*What we are today comes from our thoughts of yesterday,
and our present thoughts build our life of tomorrow:
Our life is the creation of our mind.*
Buddha

CHAPTER 9 MIRROR, MIRROR   45

*As above, so below, as within, so without,
as the universe, so the soul.*
Hermes Trismegistus

CHAPTER 10 VICTIM VICTIMIZER   53

*The fault, dear Brutus, is not in our stars,
But in ourselves...*
William Shakespeare

CHAPTER 11 CHANGING THE PAST   61

*The past, like the future, is indefinite and exists only
as a spectrum of possibilities.*
Stephen Hawking

CHAPTER 12 UNRAVELLING PATTERNS   67

*There is an expiry date on blaming your parents for
steering you in the wrong direction; the moment you are
old enough to take the wheel, responsibility lies with you.*
J.K. Rowling

CHAPTER 13 SELF-AWARENESS   74

*Rather than being your thoughts and emotion,
Be the awareness behind them.*
Eckhart Tolle

CHAPTER 14 FORGIVENESS   78

We must develop and maintain the capacity to forgive. He who is devoid of the power to forgive is devoid of the power to love. Darkness cannot drive out darkness; only light can do that. Hate cannot drive out hate; only love can do that.
                    Martin Luther King, Jr.

CHAPTER 15 GRATITUDE   86

If the only prayer you ever say is Thank you, that is enough.
                    Meister Eckhart

CHAPTER 16 RELEASE   89

You empower what you fight.
You withdraw power from what you release.
                    Alan Cohen

CHAPTER 17 REPLACEMENT   99

When we quit thinking primarily about ourselves and our own self-preservation, we undergo a truly heroic transformation of consciousness.
                    Joseph Campbell

CHAPTER 18 LOVE   103

All my life, my heart has yearned for a thing I cannot name.
                    Andre Breton

CHAPTER 19 INTO THE UNKNOWN   110

As you move outside of your comfort zone, what was once the unknown and frightening becomes your new normal.
                    Robin S. Sharma

CHAPTER 20 REMINDERS   113

The True Self is not our creation, but God's. It is the self we are in our depths. It is our capacity for divinity and transcendence.
                    Sue Monk Kidd

INTRODUCTION

This above all: to thine own self be true,
And it must follow, as the night the day,
Thou canst not then be false to any man.
William Shakespeare

When I was a little girl, I prayed for a magic pill, one that would fast freeze the world exactly as it was. The world I knew was perfect and if things would stay the way they were, I would be happy forever. No such pill was invented. I grew up and discovered that the world was not perfect after all. Sadly, neither was I.

Perhaps it was the memory of my idyllic childhood that set me on the path my life followed: searching for the peace, security and love I had once known. Or perhaps that memory of real happiness had roots in a different dimension of reality. At any rate, I hungered to recapture it. What I eventually came to understand is that I was seeking my True Self. That's what we all long for whether or not we realize it.

My personal quest for Self knowledge led to extensive metaphysical and spiritual studies long before the subjects were as popular as they are today. Learning of my interest, people began asking me for information and advice. At their urging, I eventually put together a few seminars and things gradually snowballed from there. I have now been studying and teaching these subjects for 40 years. My classes, lectures and workshops are a way of sharing what I have learned, as is this book.

Over the years, I worked with many people in groups and individually. The stories in this book are fictional composites of their stories. While our lives may differ greatly on the surface, inside we are very much the same. We all seek happiness and love, a sense of completion and fulfillment. I believe what we yearn for can only be had by reuniting with our True Self. My goal is to help you in achieving that.

PLEASE NOTE:

Have pen and paper available to do the processes. Writing taps into different areas of the brain and reveals more than merely thinking about responses.

Although the words mind and brain are generally used interchangeably in this book, mind is much more than brain. The brain is a part of mind, a subdivision or channel of it.

The words feeling and emotion are used interchangeably in this book.

CONNECTION KEYS

At the end of each chapter, there will be a key to help you in unlocking the door to your True Self.

CHAPTER 1

WHO ARE YOU?

All the world's a stage,
And all the men and women merely players;
They have their exits and their entrances,
And one man in his time plays many parts...
William Shakespeare

In the journey of life, we all play many parts. We also lose parts of ourselves along the way. We come to believe that we are not okay as we are, and aspects of our nature get pushed aside and denied. Perhaps we draw that conclusion from the way we were raised. Or maybe we were taught the doctrine of original sin and think we were born guilty. Advocates of reincarnation believe we carry misperceptions about life and self from other lives into this one. Possibly the dark side of human nature is in the genes. In his book "Dark Nature," biologist Lyall Watson proposes three laws of all genes:

1. Be nasty to outsiders.
2. Be good to insiders.
3. Cheat whenever possible.

Distasteful as those laws sound, all organisms have had to rely on them to survive, and that includes human beings. Outsiders are not to be trusted; they might take something from us or hurt us. They could invade our territory, steal our food, kill us. Law 1 is a 'do unto them before they do unto you' dictum. On the other hand, it behooves us to be good to insiders, those within our tribe, family, community. We need their help and support. Finally, we are all essentially selfish and cheating can enable us to get what we want, need, feel entitled to.

As we evolved, altruism and cooperation came into the picture. When humans shifted from a nomadic to an agricultural, settled society, they needed to get along with a greater number and wider range of people. Altruism and cooperation were beneficial to survival. Those impulses developed in our nature in addition to the three basic instincts of the genes. We remained fearful of outsiders, suspicious of other races, religions and cultures. We continued to favor our own, and do what needed to be done to get what we wanted. However, we learned to cloak baser impulses and instincts in more acceptable behaviors.

As we evolved, so did our moral instincts. We learned that courtesy, helpfulness and reciprocation brought more rewards than cheating and stealing. Well, most of us did. There are still plenty of thieves, scam artists and psychopaths among us. Though hidden and modified in the rest of us, the dark nature still exists and shows itself in various guises and in certain circumstances. Wherever this dark nature – what Carl Jung called the shadow self – comes from, the result is the same: we all believe there is something deeply, inherently and irreparably wrong with us. It must be kept hidden.

The person we choose to be automatically creates a dark double –the person we choose not to be. Thomas Moore

We hide the dark double behind façades we develop.

Persona means mask and the false self has many masks. We become actors, don different costumes, play different roles: parent, partner, child, worker, friend, teacher, student, on and on. We are constantly changing our façade/face depending on the people, times, situations we're involved in. Consider all the different facets of personality people have: serious, funny, critical, compassionate, judgmental, dominating, submissive, demanding, easy going. There is no permanent, fixed personality. Forty-three facial muscles produce thousands of expressions enabling us to have a different face for every occasion: cheerful, irritated, shy, sad, arrogant, determined, sneaky, to name a few.

We recreate ourselves moment to moment. We change instant to instant depending upon our thoughts, emotions, experience and the energy around us. Different people call forth different aspects of our nature just as we do theirs. After a while, we're not sure who we really are. In a desperate drive to define ourselves – to feel real – we develop specialized personalities, talents, relationships, works, possessions and so on. But still, the question lingers in the back of our minds: Who am I?

PROCESS

1. Complete this statement with as many words as possible:

I am _____.

EXAMPLES: I am a woman, wife, daughter, mother, friend, cook, gardener, accountant, tennis player…

2. Complete this statement with as many words as possible:

At various times, I am _____.

EXAMPLES: angry, anxious, happy, funny, serious, sick, healthy...

You are, in fact, none of what you mentioned. Your words do not define you. They describe your various roles and experiences. We have all been hypnotized to believe we are what we do and the face we present the world. We know ourselves only as the costume we're wearing, but behind it there is a deep seated anxiety that none of it is real. We sense the façade will crack and fall apart the minute we stop reinforcing it, so we put all our efforts into shoring it up, dressing it up, making it stronger, more special. And still the sense persists: this is not who I truly am. When we finally admit it, the search for Self begins. We confront the perennial, existential question, "Who am I?"

THE TRUE SELF IS WHO WE WOULD BE WITHOUT THE NEGATIVE FILTERS AND MISPERCEPTIONS THAT DISTORT PURE LIFE ENERGY.

This book will help you remove those filters and misperceptions and re-discover your True Self. It will explain how the life force gets stifled and twisted, and provide means for detecting and dismantling the blocks that keep you from feeling wholly, happily alive in the present. The degree to which you desire wholeness will determine the speed of your journey.

A drunk was stumbling through a cemetery one night when he fell into a newly dug grave. The walls were muddy and slippery. Try as he did, he couldn't climb out. A while later another man, taking a short cut home from work after dark, was crossing the cemetery and fell in the same hole. Out of the totally black night came the drunk's voice, "Once you fall in here, you can't get out." But the man did.

The drunk didn't have the energy or motivation to climb out but the second man, thinking he was in hell, did. When pain or unhappiness is great enough, we will discover resources we didn't know we had and have the power to climb out.

CONNECTION KEY 1: Write a description of your ideal self. What would you be like?

CHAPTER 2

FALSE SELF VS. TRUE SELF

God has given you one face,
and you make yourself another.
Shakespeare

The more we deny our true identity, the emptier we feel. The emptier we feel, the more we seek comfort in food, drink, drugs, relationships, possessions. It is no secret that obesity, addictions and depression are major problems in the United States. More than 2/3 of the American adult population is overweight or obese. The best selling drugs in the country treat depression and other mental disorders.

We may be putting on a happy face, but we are not truly happy, healthy people. How can we feel secure when the self we identify with is a flimsy creation that keeps changing? How can we feel secure when we believe we're not good enough, smart enough, loveable enough? How can we feel secure when the dark double lingers below the surface and threatens to break through?

Fortunately, no matter what insecurities and dark impulses reside within, we have the power to transform them into positive energies. But first we have to face them. We can't heal what we refuse to acknowledge. It is in denying our thoughts and feelings, driving them out of conscious awareness that they grow into frightful, negative forces that cast a dark shadow over the True Self and stifle the flow of pure energy. Looking is the light that illuminates darkness and dispels it.

LOOKING MEANS...

Honestly acknowledging and confronting:
our dark nature
insecurity
judgments
misperceptions
unloving thoughts
repressed emotions
guilt and fear
attack impulses
investment in our roles
grievances
all Self-defeating thoughts

That is what we will be doing throughout this book – bringing the hidden self to the surface, challenging its reality, correcting misperceptions and healing emotional pain. As we dismantle the false self, our true nature will be revealed.

WE DON'T HAVE TO SEARCH FOR THE TRUE SELF.
IT WILL APPEAR WHEN WE REMOVE
INTERFERENCES TO IT.

Few people are living as their True Self in this world. Surely Jesus and Buddha did, gurus of the past and some of our present day spiritual gurus as well, like the Dalai Lama. But what about the rest of us? Why is it so hard for us? We are attached to the identities we have created. Believing the body and psyche are our only reality, we fear losing them. To drop the masquerade requires courage and faith that something better will take its place.

Answering the call of the True Self often feels like swimming across a body of water. You've heard there is something wonderful on the other side, but you can't see it. Midway across, you wonder if it is wise to give up the shore you know for one you don't. You are tempted to turn around and swim back or, torn between the two, stay in no man's land and tread water. You're not even sure exactly what you're swimming toward. What is the True Self?

While we can endeavor to describe it with words such as light, love and peace, the True Self must be experienced to be known. We have all had such experiences whether we realized it at the time or not...

When beautiful music brings tears to your eyes

When an experience touches you so deeply, you feel your heart open

When a scene in nature overwhelms you

When a pervasive sense of peace comes over you

When you are immersed in a project and actions flow without thought

When you spontaneously reach out to help a stranger having no thought of recognition or reward

When you lose yourself in the silent space

When the right idea or guidance miraculously appears

When you automatically know the right words to say and actions to perform

When you share good natured and whole hearted laughter

When you look on the world with compassion
instead of judgment...

You are transcending the false self and experiencing your True Self. When that happens, we are fulfilled – literally filled full of light and love. As wonderful as that sounds, as much as we all yearn for it, we have resistance. We fear the unknown. We're attached to our individual identities and beliefs. That's why awakening is usually a gradual process. We don't disappear into a blaze of glory never to be seen again. Hearts and minds begin to open. Life is more peaceful and joyful. Our words and actions are inspired by loving kindness and we are not attached to the results of our efforts.

As we remove the layers that cover the True Self, we will have longer and deeper experiences. The great Hindu guru Ramana Maharshi said:

Realization is not acquisition of anything new nor is it a new faculty. It is only removal of all camouflage.

The false self is a fictional story we have created and laid over our True Self. Seeing through it requires patience, honesty and effort. We can move as quickly or slowly as we like. The end is guaranteed. Unlike the false self, the True Self is eternal. We did not lose it. We just need to remove the camouflage.

On the mountains of truth you can never climb in vain: either you will reach a point higher up today, or you will be training your powers so that you will be able to climb higher tomorrow. Friedrich Nietzsche

CONNECTION KEY 2: How can you begin to realize the ideal self you described in Connection Key 1?

CHAPTER 3

ENERGY PRESSES

Unexpressed emotions will never die. They are buried alive
And will come forth later in uglier ways.
Sigmund Freud

If we are to take control of our minds and lives, we need to understand how our thoughts and feelings developed, how energy got blocked and trapped inside and how we can release it.

Energy is the essence of life. The body-mind as an energy field. Thoughts are energy. Pain is energy. Emotions are e-motions: energy in motion. As waves of energy, they pass through one's energy field. Well, ideally they pass through. Sometimes emotions get stuck, unable to find a pathway out. The flow of energy is blocked and the blockage eventually creates painful effects in the body and mind.

How does energy get stuck? Imagine your energy field as a clear, open space. You have an experience – something *impresses* you, literally *presses into* your energy field. To return to a clear, unobstructed state, you have to *express* or *press out* the thoughts or feelings that *pressed in.*

A healthy newborn baby is probably the best human example of a clean, clear energy field. Babies have no problem with expression. As soon as a feeling impresses – moves into their experience – they express it. If it is a feeling of pleasure, they smile and laugh; energy is flowing freely and feels good. If babies are hungry or cold or in pain, they fuss and cry. They will cry long and loud until their needs are met. They are expressing their discomfort. Assuming the baby is loved and well cared for, needs will soon be met. Having expressed and released the pain, the baby reverts to his or her natural, contented state with no negative after effects.

To maintain a clear energy field, what goes in must come out. Express must equal impress. That is the only way to remain whole, fully energized and living in the present. Unfortunately, there are other ways to press energy. We can *repress* – press it back in, and *depress* – press it down. When that happens, the unexpressed energy gets trapped in the energy field.

Impress = press into
Express = press out
Repress = press back in
Depress = press down

When you hold your breath, eat when you're not hungry, drink too much or distract yourself in some way from what you're feeling, you are repressing energy. If you depress the energy – shove it down and hold it down – it goes into the unconscious. It is temporarily out of sight but not out of mind. In spite of our best efforts to keep it hidden, depressed energy leaks out into our bodies, feelings and behavior.

Whether you carry emotional pain from the past or hurt feelings from a recent insult, that energy is churning inside you – physically and psychologically. We pretend that not acknowledging painful feelings makes them go away, but disappearing from conscious awareness does not mean they vanish. Denied pain goes underground. As additional feelings are repressed over time, the backload grows and builds in intensity. Finally we add the proverbial straw to the camel's back and all that energy explodes like a volcano. The eruption can scald us with intense mental, emotional and physical reactions. Alternatively, it may spew its venom on other people as anger, hate or physical aggression. In some way, the internal will appear externally and create havoc.

Repression causes self-division. We deny and repress what we are not supposed to be, think and feel, and consciously act out what we think we should be. It is as if a cleaver cuts the self in two. One side we claim as me – I am this. The other side we reject – I am not that. We do this over and over during the course of a life and limit our awareness to the fragmented self we isolate on one side of the artificial psychic boundary. The irony is we are neither this self nor that self. We are the Self buried beneath them.

We know what we are, but know not what we may be.
Shakespeare

CONSCIOUS SELF – Limited, false identity

UNCONSCIOUS SELF – De-pressed pain, guilt, Self-defeating patterns

TRUE SELF – Pure, clear energy. Light, love.

The part we deny does not disappear quietly into the night. It hammers at us from within and as it grows, so does the force with which it hammers at us. As a door will bend and eventually break when a strong force repeatedly bangs against it, so too will we eventually break.

Stress is the result of holding back energy that is seeking expression and release. The longer you try to hold that door closed the greater the stress to the body. Trying to hold back the natural forward flow of energy exhausts and distorts the human body.

STRESS TEST: Hold a glass of water out in front of you. At first, it's easy but gradually it becomes uncomfortable. Your hand and arm will begin to shake. Eventually, in spite of great effort, you will not be able to hold that glass of water. So it is with our blockades against repressed energy. They eventually collapse.

Obviously, it is not always possible or appropriate to express one's feelings as they arise. There is another way to press energy that helps us in such situations. Suppressing energy means that you recognize the feeling and will deal with it but not at the present moment.

SUPPRESS = PUT ASIDE TEMPORARILY

Bill and JoAnn were having dinner with friends. In an effort to be entertaining, JoAnn told a story that made fun of Bill. He was embarrassed. Rather than make a scene in front of the other couple, Bill waited until they were home to address the situation. By then, he was not as upset and had two choices:

1. He could explain how he had felt to JoAnn without attacking her.

2. He could do one of the release processes in Chapter 16.

To suppress an emotion means we recognize the present is not the time or place to express it. The greater the emotional reaction, however, the more difficult it is to suppress. When emotion overpowers us, control goes out the window and we revert to angry children.

CONNECTION KEY 3: Honesty is the opposite of repression. Don't deny negative feelings or judgments. Admit them to yourself, look at them.

CHAPTER 4

THE ANGRY CHILD WITHIN

Anger is an acid that can do more harm to the vessel
in which it is stored than to anything on which it is poured.
Mark Twain

Very early in life we discovered that it wasn't safe to express everything we thought and felt. To receive love and approval, we had to repress certain thoughts, feelings and behavior. That led to self-division – we had to separate the acceptable self from the unacceptable self. Fear, guilt, inhibitions, manipulation are some of the effects of self-division. No wonder there is an angry child inside the hidden self.

No one got the total attention and perfect love desired. As we mature, we learn to adapt when we don't get what we want, but as children, there is only one response: anger. Just watch toddlers when a toy is taken away or things don't go their way. They scream, kick, bite, hit. Rage is the only tool they have to try control the situation. When it doesn't work, the frustration is almost unbearable.

Mature adults can usually keep a rein on their anger and the way they express it. Now and then, however, a situation will ignite a powder keg of repressed anger, and the emotional response mechanisms of a child take over.

Adults then regress and express as children throwing temper tantrums complete with screams, tears and physical aggression. The rational mind takes a backseat to the emotional, irrational child within. That's why arguing with an angry person is like arguing with a child or a drunk – reason cannot be heard.

Some children have better childhoods than others and don't have as deep a well of anger. But if the right buttons are pushed in just about anyone, an angry child will come forth. When that happens, we blame the present situation for causing the anger when, in fact, it merely triggers what was already within us.

Whether overtly vicious or passively aggressive, anger is an attack, an effort to control, make another person feel guilty or in some way pay for our pain. It never resolves anything. Why? Anger is a secondary emotion, a defense against deeper, more painful feelings.

THE PAIN IS HIDDEN BEHIND THE ANGER

PROCESS

1. Think of someone or something that arouses your anger. Fill in the blanks: I am angry at or about _____ for (the reason)
_____.

EXAMPLE: I am angry at Company XYZ for not returning my phone call.

The experience in itself is neutral. What's upsetting is your interpretation of what it means.

INTERPRETATION CAUSES EMOTION

2. How does that situation/person make you feel?

_____.

EXAMPLE: Not having my call returned makes me feel rejected, ignored, unimportant.

Now those are painful feelings. They can leave you weak and depressed. Anger feels energizing in comparison to that! It's invigorating to let off steam, but the satisfaction is momentary. Attacking others with anger actually compounds emotional pain and problems rather than healing them. Anger has damaging effects on the body, brain and relationships.

To rise above the reactions of an angry child, we need to recognize that we are the cause of our anger, not other people or events. It is our interpretation that sparks anger, not the situation itself.

PROCESS

By making a situation okay, we neutralize interpretation and thereby diffuse anger. That enables us to see the situation anew, as adults. We can then make rational, constructive choices.

1. Make your upsetting incident okay.

EXAMPLE: It's okay that Company XYZ did not return my phone call.

Keep repeating that statement until you feel emotions settle down.

2. What can you do about the situation?

EXAMPLE: Call again? Write a letter? Contact

someone else?

In some situations, saying "It's okay," can instantly dispel irritation. Your spouse/child/boss failed to thank you for something? It's okay. You forgot an item at the grocery store? It's okay. Lost the tennis match? It's okay. Just saying those words can keep you from making a big deal out of inconsequential things.

Of course, some situations are not okay. Terrorism is not okay. Murder is not okay. Cancer is not okay. In such cases, make your feelings okay...

> EXAMPLE: It's okay to be angry about terrorism. It's okay to fear cancer.

While it's okay to have anger and fear, what are you going to do to move beyond them? If you can change something you don't like, change it. If you can't change it, you need to change yourself. Otherwise, the ongoing effects of anger or fear will take a terrible toll. Future chapters provide processes for changing perception and releasing emotional pain. For now, practice saying, "It's okay," to the little daily disturbances that don't warrant your attention and emotion.

Anger is a roadblock that forbids passage to the True Self. As we unravel our patterns, we will respond to upsets in positive, constructive ways. First, let's see how those patterns were formed.

CONNECTION KEY 4: Take responsibility for your anger. When something upsets you, say, "I thought this person/situation made me angry (annoyed, irritated) but I choose my feelings."

CHAPTER 5

WEAVING PATTERNS

Your visions will become clear only when you can look into your own heart. Who looks outside, dreams; who looks inside, awakes.
C.G. Jung

As a child begins to walk and talk, full, uninhibited expression is usually discouraged. Parents/caretakers say things like, "No! Stop! Not now. What's wrong with you? Good boys/girls don't do that." If we continue to behave as we did in the past, we may actually begin to suffer for what has, to date, been acceptable. Actions that brought beneficial results can receive disapproval, even punishment. Whereas crying once elicited comforting, it now results in being sent to our room, or we're warned, "Keep that up and you'll have something to cry about."

Obviously we all need to learn how to behave in this world in order to survive and thrive. The manner in which we learn those lessons, however, can encourage or stunt growth. The way parents deal with a child's experiences, behavior and emotions establishes positive or negative patterns that have lifelong effects.

A dog bite could create a permanent fear of dogs, but it doesn't have to. For children to overcome any fear, they should be encouraged to talk about their experience, thoughts and feelings. Talking releases energy. Once the initial upset has subsided, education regarding the object of fear can reduce it. In the case of a dog bite, helpful techniques are telling stories and showing videos about dogs, providing the opportunity to play with puppies. Let children move at their own pace, praise progress and confidence will gradually build. If things are dealt with correctly as they occur, energy will not be repressed and have negative effects later. Ignoring or making light of a child's fears compounds emotional trauma.

Children's feelings are very fragile. Being reprimanded, insulted, ridiculed, ignored is just as hurtful to them as it is to adults. Actually, more so. As adults, we can rationalize or reject another's words. Children can't rationalize or analyze until the age of 7 or 8. Prior to that point, everything goes in without filters to separate true from false, right from wrong, and logical from illogical. Many of our perceptions about ourselves, life and other people can be traced back to things we heard during our childhood.

Children's brains are fertile ground; ideas take root quickly and grow. Those ideas can be completely irrational because they were taken literally. A friend of mine went clothes shopping for her five year old. When she got home, she handed him a bag with several new outfits and said, "Here, Chris, go put these on." Some time passed before Chris shuffled out of his room in tears. He could hardly move. He was wearing all the new clothes.

Little ones believe exactly what they are told: that they are bad, stupid, clumsy, smart, loveable or any other message they repeatedly receive. They draw conclusions and form perceptions based on what they hear and see, and the way they are treated. Those conclusions may be faulty or downright wrong but they dig deep grooves in the neural pathways of the brain and establish patterns of thought and behavior. They dictate perception and color the self-image.

Not being listened to, comforted when hurt or acknowledged in positive ways is hurtful at any age but can have lifelong effects for a child. Repeated messages like "Good girls/boys don't do that" distort perception of what it means to be female or male. A boy who is repeatedly told and/or punished for crying may never shed tears, and be critical of any man who does. A girl who is repeatedly rebuked or punished for aggressive behavior may grow up afraid to assert herself in any situation. I say 'repeatedly' because correction when warranted isn't going to damage a child nor is the occasional misguidance of parents who are primarily loving and supportive.

It is not just DNA we receive from our parents. Prejudiced people raise prejudiced children. Immoral people raise immoral children. We mimic parental behavior and parrot their opinions. Even as mature adults, people often feel guilty if they go against the religion or political party of their parents. Until we become rational, thinking, self-determining adults, we are subject to countless influences that weave patterns in the subconscious that affect our thoughts, emotions and behavior.

Cathy grew up repeatedly hearing, "Money is the root of all evil." The actual words are, "For the love of money is a root of all kinds of evil." (1 Timothy 6:10 English Standard Version) Unfortunately, Cathy never heard the correct version. She grew up believing money is the root of all evil, so she was afraid of it. Beliefs don't exist in isolation. They have tendrils – other beliefs attached to them. Cathy also believed her parents' would disapprove of her, God would punish her and other people would be jealous and dislike her if she had money. Consequently, she unconsciously sabotaged opportunities for job promotions and the opportunity to make more money.

Fortunately, Cathy didn't have to deal with all those beliefs individually. She just had to dismantle the root cause. Upon seeing the actual quote in the Bible, Cathy realized she could be financially successful and still be religious. Her fears about God's punishment, disappointing her parents and not being a likable person dissolved concurrently.

The patterns of belief and behavior that are woven in childhood will have effects until subjected to the rational thinking of an adult.

PROCESS

1. What negative messages did you repeatedly receive as a child? Consider messages received verbally, by the way you were treated, by observing your parents and the home environment.

EXAMPLE: Talking back is unacceptable.

2. How are those messages affecting you now?

EXAMPLE: I don't stand up for myself.

I think it's very important that you make your own decision about what you are. Therefore you're responsible for your actions, so you don't blame other people.
Prince William

CONNECTION KEY 5: Look at your beliefs and values. Which are the result of adult thinking and choices, and which ones are carry-overs from childhood?

CHAPTER 6

THE PAST IS PRESENT

The human body is the best picture of the human soul.
Ludwig Wittgenstein

We carry the past with us. Not just in our memories but in our bodies – bones and muscles, blood and cells, intestines and hearts. Repressed energy is alive and potent, affecting physiology, attitudes and behavior. The pain of the past casts its shadow on the present. Sometimes it can be seen in posture and the way we walk – stooped shoulders, no pep in the step. Sometimes it shows on the face – frown lines and empty eyes. Sometimes it comes out in words – cold, critical. And sometimes the pain of the past appears as chronic physical problems or illness. Clichés tell the tale...

> Broken hearted...Cold hearted...Heart ache...Bad
> blood...Head ache...Sore throat...Weak
> kneed...Stomach ache...Pain in the neck...Thin
> skinned...Not a leg to stand on

The body reflects the way we see ourselves, pain we carry from the past and the effects of stress. It develops hard spots and contortions from holding depressed energy down but it trickles out. A mood comes over us or we feel anxious and don't know why or we lash out at people for no apparent reason. Or we get sick. Serious illness can be the effect of many factors – internal and external – that combine over a period of time.

What goes on in the mind comes out in the body. People who suffer from multiple personality disorder are proof that psychological changes cause physical changes. Individual personalities inhabiting the same body exhibit different physiology. One personality may have perfect eyesight while another needs glasses; some have allergies, others do not. As the psyche of the body hosting the multiple personalities changes, so do physical effects.

Bodies as well as personalities shape themselves around experience and beliefs. Andrew was a good worker but every promotion passed him by. He was well liked but wasn't considered management material because he couldn't make a decision. He was *unable to take a stand*. As a child of divorce, Andrew was torn between his parents. He tried to please both, aligned himself with the parent he was with at the moment. He had *a foot in both camps*, fearful of losing the affection and approval of either parent. Andrew grew up to be a people pleaser. He had difficulty *standing up* for himself or taking one side or the other when a decision had to be made. Andrew developed chronic problems with his feet.

Aside from having physical effects, mental and behavioral patterns that were laid down many years ago continue to dictate perceptions and reactions. Not all were detrimental. It is good to know that fire burns and crimes invoke punishment. What is detrimental is harboring repressed fear, guilt and anger, and perceiving the present through the lens of the past. Our upbringing may have led us to conclude that life is good or scary, people are kind or cruel, we are lovable or not. Those conclusions determine the way

32

we see ourselves and the world.

What can we do about the beliefs that cause hurtful emotions and behavior? We've all heard… "Let the past go, live in the present. Forgive and forget. S/he isn't worth it. Get on with your life. You can always buy another dog." Not only do sentiments like these not help, they are insensitive and can actually increase suffering. If we could forgive and forget, we would. But we can't. Why not? Because our wounds are deep and rooted in the unconscious. Conscious efforts barely touch them.

Fortunately, we don't have to go digging into the past to unearth the roots of our symptoms, perceptions and emotions. Present experiences are tuning forks that resonate corresponding energy within. Every time Andrew had to take a stand and make a decision, depressed anxiety and fear came rushing to the surface. The present conflict opened the door to repressed energy providing an opportunity to work with it and challenge the beliefs that were immobilizing him.

PERCEPTIONS, EMOTIONS AND PHYSICAL ISSUES ARE KEYS TO LOCKED DOORS OF THE PAST

Providing a positive outlet for what we feel in the present allows corresponding pent up energy escape as well. Future chapters will provide ways to do that. In the meantime…

CONNECTION KEY 6: BREATHE! Energy moves on the breath. The more we repress feelings, the shallower breathing becomes. When emotions and stress arise, pause, breathe deeply and tell your body to relax.

CHAPTER 7

PASSION & ADDICTION

*If a person is to get the meaning of life he must learn to like
the facts about himself – ugly as they may seem to his
sentimental vanity – before he can learn
the truth behind the facts.*
Eugene O'Neill

Daily life is filled with little setbacks. Things don't always go as we wish or expect. Efforts are unappreciated; we take offense at something someone says. These jabs and disappointments disturb us but that's life, right? We tend to ignore them and carry on. Repressed emotion from all those little injuries can build up inside and eventually overload us physically, mentally and emotionally. Despite our best efforts to keep the energy pressed down, it breaks through and flares out of control. Unfortunately, when we explode – internally or externally – the relief is short lived. Pent up energy isn't released; it's just letting off steam. Steam scalds and temporary relief gives way to embarrassment and guilt.

It's the same with addictions. They give temporary relief; that's why we are addicted. They are also destructive leaving humiliation and guilt in their wake. The word addiction means craving and dependency. The word passion is generally interpreted to mean strong desire but originally, it meant to suffer. Put addiction and passion together and you have a dependency on that which makes you suffer.

Addiction and passion can have roots in childhood. People who were sorely deprived of approval, nurturing, attention, material comforts are inclined to develop a passionate desire for those things. The method used to obtain the object of desire is the addiction.

PASSION IS THE DESIRE, ADDICTION THE MEANS

Roger had rheumatic heart as a child. His over-protective mother kept him home after school, treated him as a weak invalid. Greatly frustrated and fighting against the image his mother held of him, he left home as soon as he could. He was passionate about proving his masculinity. Roger took jobs that involved hard, physical labor and risk taking. He developed an addiction to dangerous adventures. Eventually it led to his downfall and he became the weak, helpless person his mother perceived.

There are empty places in us that ignite passionate cravings. We become addicted to anything that promises to fill the empty places and ease our pain. We look outside for what's lacking inside. Our whole society is suffering a sense of lack reflected in a passion for power, fame, money, material goods with addictions to sex, work, food, possessions, drugs, alcohol.

Passion and addiction are powerful forces. They release chemicals in the brain that excite and motivate us. The lustful passion felt at the outset of romantic relationships releases chemicals that have effects similar to cocaine and heroin, and are just as addictive. So called love addicts love to be in love but never are. They want the lusty passionate feeling, not the person. Of course, that high doesn't last – no high does – so another must be found to feed the addiction.

We can all relate to the desire for love. The problem is that people who were deprived of love were likely to conclude that they are unworthy of it. As much as they long for it, they cannot accept it. Some have sexual relationships but no intimate ones. Others drive partners away when they get too close. Some avoid personal relationships altogether. People who were physically abused as children may be addicted to abusive partners because they believe that's the price they must pay for love.

The problem is not past experiences, but beliefs resulting from them. Our minds seek, find and produce what we believe not what we want. We attract relationships and experiences that reinforce unconscious beliefs – not conscious desires.

UNCONSCIOUS BELIEFS OVERPOWER CONSCIOUS DESIRES

Satisfying our passion offers temporary relief at best. If separated from parents for long periods of time, we may fear abandonment and seek partners who promise never to leave us. In time, our neediness and smothering drive them away and we relive the anguish of abandonment. Were needs ignored as mother attended to other siblings? That can cause feelings of deprivation and the belief that there isn't enough for you. Unless the need from the past is addressed and the pain and patterns around it released, the compensation will fail. In the end, we relive the original experience as Roger did.

NOTE: One can't presume to know a person based on their health, passions etc. People respond to the imprints of childhood in different ways. This book is about developing greater self-awareness, not analyzing others. Only you can connect the dots from your past to the present.

PROCESS

   1. Fill in the blank: I am a _____aholic

   EXAMPLES: Workaholic, alcoholic, foodaholic, controlaholic, healthaholic. (Anything can become an addiction – sex, shopping, fitness, clothes, books).

   2. What need does your addiction satisfy?

   EXAMPLES: Work makes me feel important, worthwhile, needed. Alcohol/drugs make me feel happy, carefree. Food comforts me. Control makes me feel strong, safe. Health makes me feel ageless.

   Your answers are your passions: importance, happiness, comfort, safety, youth.

Lucy was an alcoholic. Without the inhibition freeing effects of alcohol, Lucy was shy, introverted and, in her words, 'gutless.' With a few drinks under her belt, she was outgoing and fun, an adventurer. Or so she thought. When her friends staged an intervention, she discovered that they didn't see her that way. What they saw was a sloppy, silly drunk whose behavior was careless and at times dangerous.

Lucy was using alcohol to compensate for shyness rather than face the causes and learn healthy ways to overcome them. With the help of rehab and counseling, Lucy learned that her shyness was actually a mask over an inferiority complex. She didn't *like* the ugly facts about herself as Eugene O'Neill (no relationship) suggested in his quote at the beginning of this chapter, but she did have to accept them in order to overcome them.

WE CAN'T HEAL WHAT WE DON'T ACCEPT

Self-discovery is an exciting journey but not an easy one. We are not going to like everything we learn about ourselves. There are ugly emotions within human beings. If we're honest, we will find them within ourselves. We all have a strong streak of selfishness. We manipulate to get what we want. We can be controlling, judgmental, self-righteous and insensitive. Welcome the dark side when it appears because we can't heal what we deny. Looking at the hidden self is like opening a closet we think holds dark and scary forces. But when the door opens, all that happens is dust escapes and junk falls out.

Every pain, addiction, anguish, longing, depression, anger or fear is an orphaned part of us seeking joy, some disowned shadow wanting to return to the light.
Jacob Nordby

CONNECTION KEY 7: What do you crave and why? What is the feeling you want or the pain you are trying to kill?

CHAPTER 8

THOUGHT – EMOTION – ACTION

What we are today comes from our thoughts of yesterday,
and our present thoughts build our life of tomorrow:
Our life is the creation of our mind.
Buddha

We have thousands and thousands of thoughts every day. Most flitter through the brain with no effects because a thought in itself has a low vibratory rate. It is energized by attention. The more you dwell on a thought, the more energy you feed it. When the vibration becomes strong enough, it can be felt. The thought has transformed into e-motion: energy in motion. That energy will seek an outlet through verbal or physical action.

Thoughts are commands to energy. Think of your brain as a factory with millions of willing workers. You are the CEO and you issue directives via your thoughts. But there are so many thoughts. Which ones do the workers follow? The ones that stand out in red letters and bold print. In other words, the ones you truly believe, the ones injected with energy via conviction, contemplation, expectation and emotion. These are the thoughts that have formed neural patterns in your brain, the ones the workers obey.

Where your focus goes, energy flows. This concept is crucial to taking control of your thoughts and life. The thoughts you focus on garner the most energy and create belief systems. The workers in the brain see belief systems as blueprints upon which you wish to build your life. Those are the concepts they take seriously and set out to manifest. Their goal is to produce emotions, actions and experiences that match those blueprints. With each successful reproduction, the belief system grows stronger.

You are today where your thoughts have brought you;
you will be tomorrow where your thoughts take you.
James Allen

WE FIND WHAT WE LOOK FOR.
WE EXPERIENCE WHAT WE EXPECT.

But wait, you may say, "I didn't want to get sick. I wasn't thinking about that." Neither was Louis but he woke up one morning and felt a little sluggish. He remained in bed reviewing what he had for dinner the night before, wondering if something disagreed with him. Or had he picked up a bug at the supermarket yesterday? He got out of bed feeling achy, took some aspirin and extra Vitamin C. He expected to have a long, trying day at work. By the time Louis got to the office, he looked pale and everyone asked if he was sick. "Aha," Louis thought, "I really am sick. It's not my imagination. Everyone sees it." Louis went home and back to bed.

Louis may not have wanted to get sick – or did he? Perhaps there was something at work he didn't want to deal with. Whatever the reason, sickness is where he chose to put his focus. His wife, on the other hand, though she awoke with the same sluggish feelings, focused her attention in a different direction. She thought about the new account she had won and was excited about working on it. She got out of bed, took a shower and had a healthy breakfast. She headed off to work feeling fine and had a very productive day.

Feelings don't arise out of nowhere. They are thoughts that reached a vibratory level strong enough to be felt. They signal what is going on in the mind. Positive thoughts generate positive emotions that release feel good chemicals in the brain and body. Negative thinking has poisonous effects. Loving thoughts open the energy field and allow more energy to flow to us and through us. Fearful thoughts contract the energy field blocking the full, free flow of energy causing painful physical and emotional feelings. Many thoughts are inconsequential and drop away. Others are energized and become feelings that inspire action.

PROCESS

1. I feel _____ because I think
_____.

EXAMPLE: I feel worried because I think I can't pay my bills.

2. Worry causes me to (act or react)
_____.

EXAMPLE: Worry causes me to drink. OR Worry makes me cut back on spending, cash a bond, get a second job.

Actions and reactions are not set in stone. They can be positive or negative depending on our choice. Louis and his wife experienced the same stimulus upon awakening but they chose to focus on different scenarios. Consequently, they had very different experiences. At any point along the pathway of Thought-Emotion-Action, we have...

THE POWER OF CHOICE

Today, we're overwhelmed with a plethora of choices – so many gadgets, cars, colors, clothes, books, television channels! Restaurant menus take half an hour to read. Choices such as these are inconsequential compared to the power we have to choose our reality. We all live in our own little worlds – literally – and reality like beauty is in the eye of the beholder. The thoughts, emotions and actions we choose determine the way we experience ourselves, others and the world. It's like a magic show. Change your mind, and *snap!* perceptions, feelings and experiences change. How can that be?

Let's take a peek at quantum physics – in the most simplified terms possible. Quantum physics (also known as quantum mechanics) studies energy at the atomic and subatomic level. According to its principles, there are countless waves of probability – different possible scenarios that could unfold in life. Our choices determine which ones manifest, materialize, take form. Does that mean I can choose to have a million dollars and it will appear? Sadly, no. The term is waves of *probability*. Past choices and actions determine what is presently possible.

BUT PRESENT CHOICES CAN ACTIVATE A WHOLE NEW SET OF PROBABILITIES!

Isn't that exciting? Observation is the key. Haven't you ever wondered how two different studies of the same thing can produce entirely different results? The researchers were looking for different results! There is no objective reality. We see what we're looking for. Every garage sale is proof that one man's trash is another man's treasure. People looking at the same object, experiencing the same event, meeting the same person can have entirely different perceptions and experiences.

THE BRAIN SEEKS & FINDS
WHAT IT'S LOOKING FOR

Years ago, I was giving a lecture to a group of nurses at a hospital. One asked how to deal with a particularly difficult, nasty patient. The nurse sitting next to her said, "Who are you talking about?" When the name was whispered, the second nurse was shocked. "Are you kidding? He is the sweetest man. I love him."

I often wondered how they experienced the patient the next day. Both nurses could have maintained their original opinion; people will forfeit peace and happiness in favor of believing they are right. On the other hand, each nurse could have been influenced by her colleague's opinion or what I proceeded to say, and changed her perception. The next question is: If the nurse's perception of the patient changed, did he change? We'll address that in the next chapter.

If we don't practice awareness and exert our power of choice, our lives run on automatic pilot. Our strongest thoughts dictate our perceptions, fire emotions and design our experience. We will repeat the same patterns over and over and claim we have no power over them. But we do. There is always an instant – quickly forgotten – that we choose to let a program (thought, emotion or behavior) run or not. Freedom lies in choosing. Growth comes from choosing anew. What we want to do – need to do – is catch that instant and choose again.

PROCESS: Catch yourself next time you feel annoyed. Stop, take a deep breath and remember that you have the power of choice. You can respond differently. Even if you don't like someone or something, you don't *have* to be annoyed. It is a choice.

Past programming is like a television set in the back of our minds that constantly runs the same show: the same choices, interpretations, beliefs, emotions and experience. We think we have no control over the show that's playing, but we do. We pretend our emotions come out of nowhere, but they don't. We imagine perception is reality but it's not. We see what we want to see, and we want to see evidence of what we already believe. It's like a carousel we can't get off. But we can. Choose again.

NEVER UNDERESTIMATE THE POWER OF YOUR CHOICES. FROM THEM, REALITY MANIFESTS AND FUTURE PATHWAYS OPEN

CONNECTION KEY 8: Next time a strong emotion arises, observe the thought behind it and the action it is leading to.

CHAPTER 9

MIRROR, MIRROR EVERYWHERE

As above, so below, as within, so without,
as the universe, so the soul.
Hermes Trismegistus

In the last chapter, we met two nurses who had strikingly different perceptions of the same patient. You've probably had a similar experience. Perhaps you and your partner met someone at a party. On the way home, you say, "Wasn't Joe a nice guy? So interesting. Wouldn't mind getting to know him better." And your partner replies, "Are you kidding? How could you be taken in by that guy? What a phony."

Who is right in these cases? Both are. We all look through a unique pair of glasses, so we see people and the world through different filters. Like the nurses, you and your partner's perception is based on subjective reality not objective. What you see is true for you. What your partner sees is true for him or her.

A man was appointed County Circuit Judge. He was determined to be the fairest, most open-minded judge imaginable. His first case was a dispute between neighbors regarding a boundary line. As the first man pleaded his case, the judge kept nodding and saying, "That's right. That's right." When the second neighbor had a chance to tell his side of the story, the judge was equally swayed. He nodded repeatedly and said, "Yes, that's right, that's right." The officer of the court was impelled to lean over and whisper in the judge's ear, "Sir, they can't both be right." "Oh," the judge replied, "That's right."

Everyone is right from their own perspective. We cannot truly understand another unless we put aside our glasses and look through theirs. Until we are able to do that, we can learn a lot about ourselves and the hidden content of our minds by being aware of our projections.

The popular opinion is 'seeing is believing' but the truth is believing is seeing. We literally see our thoughts reflected back to us. When we look at another person we do not experience that person. We experience our thoughts and feelings about that person.

First impressions offer one of the best examples of projection. Since they are formed in a matter of seconds, they cannot possibly be based upon the true nature and essence of a person. In fact, they are primarily based on appearance. We have positive impressions of people whose appearance we like, approve of and relate to. We react negatively if we don't like one's appearance.

First impressions are unconscious, automatic reactions. They happen before we have time to rationally assess a person or situation. Princeton psychologist Alex Todorov explains it this way: "We decide very quickly whether a person possesses…traits we feel are important…even though we have not exchanged a single word with them. It appears we are hard-wired to draw these inferences in a fast, unreflective way."

PROCESS: To demonstrate how quickly you form an

impression, look through a magazine. Stop at each clear picture of a person and notice your visceral reaction. Would you like to know this person? Why or why not? You can do the same thing with people who appear on television. Notice how you take an instant dislike to an image. Become aware of how quickly you evaluate, judge, label and react to people based strictly on appearance. We are actually reacting to what we project on people. That's why first impressions tell us more about ourselves than the people we meet.

Beyond conscious awareness, energies harmonize or clash for various reasons...

Memories influence us: I dislike this woman because she reminds me of Aunt Mary and I didn't like Aunt Mary.

We project prejudice: we dislike people of a different color or religion or political party etc.

We project our dark side: she looks sneaky.

We project our values: he's not of my class, not worth knowing.

We project expectations: I heard about you and knew we would get along.

We project our mood: we are more accepting when we are in a good mood.

We project repressed feelings: the nurse who had a negative impression of the patient could have been projecting irritation with her spouse onto him.

Everything that irritates us about others can lead us to an understanding about ourselves. Carl Jung

If a person arouses a negative response in us, it is because negative energy has been resonated. Rather than deal with what's coming up and heal it, we project it out. Now we see our repressed guilt or selfishness or weakness out there. We think the fault is in them, not us; we maintain the illusion of innocence.

It is difficult to grasp this concept if we apply it solely to form. Perhaps you see a story about a murderer on television. You react strongly to the killer, hope he gets the greatest punishment possible. That can't possibly be a mirror for you; you've never murdered anyone. But wait, look at the content of murder – destroying, eradicating – can you relate to that? Have you ever *wanted* to kill someone? Have you ever crushed someone's spirit or damaged their reputation? Maybe you project your murderous thoughts onto fictional characters in books or movies, or people in the news. Didn't you just hope that the murderer you saw on television gets put to death?

What we really want to kill is the dark side of ourselves, the part we have repressed and deemed bad, unworthy of love. Rather than confront the negative energy within us, we dissociate from it and project hateful thoughts and feelings onto externals. Then we want to reject or destroy the object we projected on. Projection would be a nice way to get rid of repressed thoughts and emotions if it worked, but it doesn't.

THE PROBLEM WITH PROJECTION

1. Projection makes repressed feelings and thoughts appear outside us but doesn't get rid of them.

2. The repressed energy can't be healed because we deny its true source (us).

3. Projection seems to justify feelings of hate and attack. Those feelings increase guilt.

4. Because projected feelings are in us, when we think we are condemning another, we are really condemning ourselves.

Projection colors perception of everything. We project our frame of mind, repressed thoughts and feelings, and past programming onto people and the world. We fail to see and understand what is actually happening in the present and see instead a reflection of what's happening inside us. If we like the side of us that appears in the mirror at any given time, we like the external image. If we don't like the feelings that come up, we don't like what we're looking at. It is always what is going on in our own mind that upsets us. We react to the thoughts and judgments and images in our mind.

We believe that attacking or changing the external picture will make unpleasant feelings go away. Oh, we may feel better for the moment but those nasty feelings will just go underground and garner more strength. Any time we think about the disturbing person or situation, the same negative feelings will arise.

The trouble with trying to run away is that mirrors are the same everywhere you go. Author unknown

As we discover unpleasant truths about ourselves like projection, it is normal to feel guilty but that is not helpful. Guilt reinforces the idea that we are bad; obviously not our goal. Our goal is to bring the hidden self to the surface so we can heal it. To that end, projection is a most helpful tool. It shows us what is inside, what we need to acknowledge and heal. If we are honest about what we are feeling and recognize that we are responsible for it, we will not project.

HONESTY/ACKNOWLEDGEMENT IS THE OPPOSITE
OF DENIAL/REPRESSION.

PROCESS

1. Think of someone who arouses a strong reaction in you. Fill in the blanks.

I feel _____ toward_____

because I think _____.

EXAMPLE: I feel sympathy toward the homeless because I think they are poor and needy.

2. How or where in your life do you exhibit the same qualities?

EXAMPLE: I don't have enough love, appreciation, money…

OR your answers could be…

EXAMPLE: I feel disgust toward the homeless because I think they are lazy.

2. How or where in your life do you exhibit the same qualities?

EXAMPLE: I am lazy about taking care of my health.

Remember to relate to the content (neediness/laziness) not the form (homelessness).

Projection is only in effect when you have a reaction. You

may look at a homeless person without any thoughts or feelings. If you have an emotional reaction, you're projecting. You may think your reaction is positive as in feeling sympathy for the homeless but you are projecting feeling sorry for your own neediness onto him.

One can feel compassion for people without feeling the emotional pangs of sympathy. Sympathy is entering into and sharing another's pain. You think you are sharing their pain but it is actually your own that is coming up.

Remember: it is always our interpretation and reaction that upsets us, not another person or event. We should actually be grateful for anyone and anything that resonates depressed energy. They open the door to the unconscious mind so we can see what's hidden in there. Every irritation provides a chance to take back a projection and work on ourselves.

OTHERS CAN AROUSE OUR PAINFUL FEELINGS BUT THEY DON'T CREATE THEM

What happens when we withdraw our projections? Let's say the nurses approached that patient with a different perception the next day. Did the patient's behavior change? It well may have since we virtually call forth the behavior we expect from people. We send out messages with our words, tone of voice, facial expression and body language indicating what we think and how we feel about a person, and they usually respond in kind. Even when we try to hide a negative perception behind a smile and friendly tone, people sense our mood and energy, and respond to it. Nevertheless, other people are not our puppets. People we like and approach with positive feelings can sometimes be in a bad mood. As long as their mood doesn't affect ours, we're not projecting.

PROCESS: First impressions are unconscious and automatic so there is no point in denying them. But the next time you meet someone, let your initial reaction subside and try to see and hear the person without projection and judgment.

Should you really open your eyes and see, you would beholdyour image in all images.
And should you open your ears and listen, you would hear your own voice in all voices.
Kahlil Gibran

CONNECTION KEY 9: When you take an instant dislike to people, try to discern what you are projecting.

CHAPTER 10

VICTIM VICTIMIZER

The fault, dear Brutus, is not in our stars,
But in ourselves...
Shakespeare

It is human nature to blame others for our pain and problems. Even as toddlers we pretend we're faultless and point accusing fingers at siblings and playmates. I once saw a video of a 3 year old repeatedly denying that she ate the cookies even though the crumbs were all over her clothes It reminded me of the man whose wife caught him in bed with another woman. "What!?!?" he cried. "Are you going to believe me or your lying eyes?"

It's in our DNA. Adam blamed Eve. Eve blamed the snake, and we've all been looking for scapegoats (why not scapesnakes?) ever since. Every time we blame external factors for our condition, we relinquish our power. We become victims. Not because of what someone did to us but because of what we do to ourselves. We allow circumstances to dictate our thoughts, feelings and reactions. Even in the harshest of conditions, we rule the domain of our mind. Psychiatrist Viktor Frankl wrote a brilliant, moving account of his years as a prisoner in Nazi death camps in the book, "Man's Search For Meaning." He observed that those who survived found some purpose, reason to live, within that most horrific of experiences. When we give suffering meaning, it can empower instead of weaken us, drive us forward instead of backward.

Everything can be taken from a man but one thing: the last of human freedoms - to choose one's attitude in any given set of circumstances, to choose one's own way.
Viktor E. Frankl

A victim's moods and well-being are at the mercy of the weather, circumstances, other people, anything and everything but himself. Like a ship with loose sails, victims are battered by every passing wind and get nowhere. A poor captain blames the wind instead of the fact that he didn't set the sails properly and remain at the helm of his ship. Seeing ourselves as victims may temporarily mollify us but requires forfeiting the power to set the sails and steer a course out of the storm.

People with a victim consciousness attract pain and disappointment. They expect to be hurt, rejected, cheated etc., and they get what they expect. They may be miserable, but they find a perverse pleasure in being right. And there is the added benefit of the attention and sympathy victims generate. The irony is that victims turn into victimizers. One way or another, overtly or covertly, victims make others pay for their misery.

This is how the **VICTIM CYCLE** works:

REFUSAL TO ACCEPT RESPONSIBILITY FOR SELF = VICTIM

VICTIM = HELPLESS

HELPLESS = ANGRY

ANGRY = ATTACK (overt or covert)

ATTACK = FEAR & GUILT

FEAR AND GUILT = WEAK & MISERABLE

WEAK & MISERABLE = BLAME OTHERS

BLAMING OTHERS = VICTIM

AND YOU START ALL OVER AGAIN!

Judith saw herself as a victim of her husband. He was demanding, controlling and emotionally abusive. He was clearly the cause of her unhappiness. She couldn't take a job because he didn't want her to work. She didn't have friends. Her anxiety and misery weakened her immune system. She was frequently ill. It was all his fault. Rather than stand up to her husband or leave him, Judith set out to make his life as miserable as hers. She became a secret shopaholic, hiding her purchases from him, spending money faster than it came in. She purposely fed him unhealthy food. As a classic passive aggressive, Judith undermined her husband in every way possible. The victim became the victimizer.

We've all played both roles. In the following processes, you may discover qualities in yourself that are not desirable. Just remember that healing requires looking at the dark side, bringing it into the light. Later, you may wish to do the Release Process with emotions that arise.

PROCESS

1. In what ways did you feel victimized as a child?

EXAMPLES: I was punished. I didn't get what I

wanted. I was lied to. I didn't feel unconditionally loved.

2. What beliefs did you form?

EXAMPLES: People hurt me. I'm deprived. People can't be trusted. I don't deserve unconditional love.

3. What feelings attend those beliefs?

EXAMPLES: Fear, Lack, Distrust, Unworthiness

4. What attitudes and behavior developed?

EXAMPLES: I'm fearful and defensive. I cheat to get what I think I deserve. I'm suspicious. I don't expect anyone to really love me.

The problem with our beliefs is that so many were formed by the frightened, irrational mind of a child. As adults, we're still letting them dictate the story of our life. We can't take charge of our lives without challenging and changing those beliefs.

NOT ACCEPTING RESPONSIBILITY = VICTIM

ACCEPTING RESPONSIBILITY = EMPOWERMENT

By pinning blame for our problems and pain on someone or something else, we proclaim our innocence. Unfortunately, it comes at a steep price. If we're not responsible for our present state, how can we possibly change it? Dropping the victim role and taking full responsibility for our lives is difficult. After all, we didn't ask for the problems that plague us, right? Well, what if we did? What if we write the script of our lives? That is not an unrealistic idea. Many quantum physicists support the theory that life as we know it is actually a hologram our minds are projecting. Modern scientists are not the first to come up with this idea. Some eastern religions and various indigenous cultures believe that this life is an illusion, a dream, and we are the dreamer of the dream.

That theory would make us not just the star of our own movies but the writer and director as well. **NOTE**: This concept gives people no comfort if they are caught up in a frightening life story and completely unaware of the nature and power of mind. To tell someone who is suffering, "You chose this," is not only **not** helpful, it's cruel. We are not yet masters of our own universe so we should not be judging others and their experience. And those who are masters of their own universe would not dream – pun intended – of judging others.

Thinking of ourselves as the scriptwriters of our story breaks the victim cycle. While we can't control the stock market, the weather and what other people do, we are responsible for how we experience these things. The overall picture of our lives is a reflection of our beliefs, needs and choices. Whether we like the scene we're in or not, it supports the theme of our life. It proves what we believe about ourselves. The good news is we can rewrite our script at any time.

PROCESS

1. Look at your life as if it were a movie and write a synopsis of the story. Describe the overall plot and the experiences that had the greatest effect on the main character – you.

Describe major relationships and their effect. What

was the purpose of your childhood script? What kind of person did it justify you becoming?

Analyze the main character. Describe personality, behavior, general attitude. Is this character friendly, likable, introverted, extroverted, kind, selfish, demanding etc.

What are the main character's major conflicts? Fears? Successes? Failures?

In what ways does the main character play victim? Victimizer?

We love to be right. That's why we affiliate with people who think as we do, watch news commentators who echo our prejudices and attract experiences that confirm our beliefs and buttress our self-image. We design our movie to prove we're right. We put characters and scenes in to blame for our problems, support our self-image and reinforce our patterns. We need others to be the way they are so we can be the way we are. See why you set things up the way you do. Ask yourself what the scene you are presently in proves.

2. Read what you have written in #1 and then answer these questions.

What is the main theme of your life movie? What is its primary purpose? Is there a hidden agenda?

What does your story prove about life? People? You?

3. Now that you can be the conscious creator of your life, how would you like the rest of the movie to unfold?

Where do you want your story to go?

What do you want the rest of your movie to prove?

What beliefs about yourself, life and people do you need to change for the movie to go in that direction?

Obviously, there are some circumstances in our lives we can't change. Jack loved to travel. His dream was to walk away from everything and backpack his way around the world, but he was tied down by family and job. But wait, Jack had chosen to get married and have children and believed it was his responsibility to support them. If he was a victim, it was of his own choices not his family and job. Once Jack stopped blaming circumstances for feeling stuck, energy was released and Jack's perspective broadened. He realized that much of his frustration was due to not liking his job. After several months of searching, he found a position much better suited to his interests. He began watching travel shows and National Geographic programs with his family. Together they organized exciting family vacations. Jack was happier and closer to his family than he had ever been.

We make choices but don't want to be responsible for them. We look for external factors to blame for our situation or emotions. We put scapegoats in our movie. We pretend that eradicating the perceived cause of our problems will set us free. Of course, it doesn't. Only by taking responsibility, changing our minds, rewriting our scripts can we change the course of our lives. It requires commitment and effort. Perhaps most of all, patience. Beliefs form neural patterns in the brain. The longer they are held, the stronger they are, the faster they fire. But we don't have to let them run. When we stop believing and acting on old patterns, they die of malnutrition.

I am not what happened to me, I am what I choose to become. C.G. Jung

CONNECTION KEY 10: Become aware of casting blame. Don't feel guilty; we all cast blame all the time – on the government, family, co-workers – anything and everything. Just be aware of the constant tendency to blame.

CHAPTER 11

CHANGING THE PAST

*The past, like the future, is indefinite and exists
only as a spectrum of possibilities.*
Stephen Hawking

The popular belief is that the past creates the present, and that is true to some extent. But it also works the other way around: the present creates the past. That's because our present state of mind colors perception of the past. The brain only recalls highlights of an event and paints in the details to create a coherent picture. Since our present state of mind changes, the way we paint the past changes.

Memories are not factual representations of the past. They are fluid, edited and revised every time we think about them. The past changes depending upon the vantage point from which we view it. If we are in a good mood, we recall an event in one frame of mind. In a bad mood, we recall the same event differently.

Quantum physics suggests that the present actually determines the past. As you will recall, the present is the manifestation of one wave of probability out of many. Each wave of probability connects to both a past and a future. In other words, our present reality is connected to one version of the past. If we change our present mindset, we shift to a different wavelength and another version of the past will appear on the movie screen of our mind.

The past is not an objective reality. It's malleable. It changes as we change. Acquiring new information colors the lens through which we perceive the past. Imagine you are watching a movie in which the main character is poorly dressed, dirty and dealing drugs. In your opinion, this is a bad guy. As the story unfolds, you learn that this character is an undercover cop. He is a good guy. Now you approve of the way he's dressed and talks and behaves; it's all part of his cover. As your feelings about him change, your memory of him in previous scenes will change. In a sense you will write over your memories of previous scenes with the new information.

Present knowledge overlays memories and alters perception of them. Imagine that you have had several pleasant chats with the new girl at work and find her likeable. Then a co-worker shares a piece of nasty gossip about the girl. Now you recall your previous interactions with her in an entirely different light. Your memory of those chats changes dramatically. And, since we always try to make ourselves look good, you now claim that you saw evidence of her faults and were suspicious of her right from the start.

It is easy to see ourselves as victims of the past and blame it for how we feel in the present. We imagine that we are unsuccessful or unhappy or guilty or angry because of something that happened in the past but it works the other way around. We have feelings in the present and then look in our memory bank for something to blame them on.

Joe's marriage was on the verge of collapse. When he married Marci, he claimed that he wanted children, but he kept putting it off. "It's been three years now," Marci claimed. "He procrastinates about everything, and in the end, he does nothing." Joe had a multitude of excuses as to why it wasn't the right time to have children but it came down to his fear that he would fail as a father. In fact, Joe's fear of failure immobilized him in every area of life. He was afraid to try anything new for fear he would fail and be humiliated.

Joe's father was just the opposite. He was forever trying a new scheme, inventing something, laughingly claiming he was on the verge of a great breakthrough that would bring fame and fortune. None of his efforts or inventions amounted to anything. Joe's mother ridiculed her husband every step of the way and laughed at his efforts. His father died a sad man when Joe was in his early teens.

When Joe's mother repeatedly told him that he was just like his father, the adolescent in him reached the conclusion that trying new things would make him a failure and a fool; that was how he had perceived his father. He stopped trying to accomplish anything because he was afraid of failing and being humiliated. Consequently, Joe didn't really know what he was capable of. He never challenged himself. Now, the very thing he feared – failure – was descending on his marriage.

Having lost his father at an early age and recalling his mother's ridicule of him had caused Joe to perceive his father as a failure. When asked to temporarily take his mother out of the picture and focus on other memories of his father, Joe saw a man who was excited about life and found pleasure simply in exploring and creating. He had a good job and supported his family. It didn't really matter to him whether his inventions succeeded or not. He loved the challenge of making new things. It wasn't fruitless efforts that made him sad in the end. It was his wife.

When Joe changed his memory of his father, he changed himself. When he revised his past memories, he rewrote the future. With his wife's support and love, and the memory of his father's creative spirit, Joe found the courage to undertake new projects. He discovered that self-esteem comes from having the courage to try, not necessarily succeeding. Every day he read these words by Thomas Edison, "If we all did the things we are really capable of doing, we would literally astound ourselves." Joe set out to astound himself. Not a bad goal.

In writing fiction, an author must create a past that justifies the nature, behavior and experiences of a character in the present. At the same time, the writer must bear in mind where the story is going. The future s/he has in mind will have an effect on what happens to the character in the present. It is the same with the story of our lives. The past we believe in supports the story of who we are now, and leads us to probable present realities. At the same time, waves of future probabilities also affect decisions and the direction we follow in the present.

WE CAN CHANGE THE PAST BY CHANGING
THE WAY WE PERCEIVE IT

PROCESS

1. Consider a relationship from the past that you believe is still having a negative effect on you.

EXAMPLE: My father beat me.

2. How is that affecting you now?

EXAMPLE: We have a very cold relationship. I

have a lot of anger. I think I hate him.

3. Find a place where you will not be interrupted. Position two chairs across from each other, close enough that if two people were sitting in them, knees would almost touch. Sit in one chair and imagine the person involved in your memory sitting in the other. Tell that person exactly how you felt then, how you feel now, how their behavior affected you.

EXAMPLE: "How could you do that to me? I was a helpless child. You hurt me. Not just physically. You made me feel bad, unworthy of your love. I still feel you don't love me. You make me angry, really angry."

4. Once you get it all out and feel calm, change chairs. Imagine that you are the other person experiencing their thoughts and feelings. Explain their behavior, point of view and why they did what they did.

EXAMPLE: "I'm sorry. I was young. I didn't know how to be a father. My father beat me. He made me feel the same way you do. I didn't want to be like him but I guess I was. I do love you. Please forgive me."

5. Return to the other chair and sit quietly absorbing what was said. Are you able to look at the other person and the past with more understanding, perhaps even compassion?

This process can also be done with a negative memory of something you did. You would play both roles – your present self and the person you were at the time.

Joe was eventually able to do this process with his mother. When he changed positions, he got the sense that his mother felt inferior to his father. She was afraid he would succeed at his hobby, become famous and leave her. That is why she undermined his projects and put him down. When she said Joe was like his father, she actually meant it as a compliment – he was smart. "I'm not sure any of it is true," Joe said, "but that's what came to me. It makes sense and most important, it enables me to look at her with compassion instead of anger."

When you change your mind, you change your past. When you change your past, you change its effect on the present. You no longer carry the resentment or anger or guilt or fear that the previous images of the past engendered so you also change your future. To forgive is to forget because your past experience is transformed into something else entirely.

CONNECTION KEY 11: Change a negative memory. Look at it from a different angle. Seek the silver lining. What did you learn? How can you use it to grow?

CHAPTER 12

UNRAVELLING PATTERNS

In the long run, we shape our lives, and we shape ourselves. The process never ends until we die. And the choices we make are ultimately our own responsibility.
Eleanor Roosevelt

People crave attention. Witness the popularity of social media and selfies. We want to be noticed. We need to be noticed. It is crucial for human development and mental health. That's why we develop personas that will be recognized and responded to. We reject parts of ourselves, nurture others and end up with a self designed to win attention. Preferably good attention via approval and love, but any recognition will do. Every child innately knows bad attention is better than no attention. If we aren't recognized for being good, smart, helpful, funny, talented, we will seek recognition in other ways. We may be the most demanding, aggressive, meanest, loudest kid on the street.

It is devastating to people not to be recognized. That's why prolonged solitary confinement can lead to mental breakdown. One of my pet peeves is people who walk right in front of me on the sidewalk or in the supermarket – like I am not even there. And that is exactly the fear it resonates. Don't you see me? Don't I exist? Whether we seek recognition by being good or bad, it is never quite enough to quell the existential fear that perhaps we aren't real after all. Perhaps our greatest fear is that Shakespeare's words are true…

This life, which had been the tomb of his virtue and of his honour, is but a walking shadow; a poor player, that struts and frets his hour upon the stage, and then is heard no more: it is a tale told by an idiot, full of sound and fury, signifying nothing.

In the many workshops I presented and processes I led people through, the bottom line for everyone was always the same: I am not enough – not good enough, lovable enough, smart enough, attractive enough. We are always lacking in some way. No matter how much we have – love, money, attention, happiness – it is never quite enough. No matter what we do, we will never be enough or have enough if we identify with the false self. It is exactly that – false, a creation of our imagination, a shadowy fragment of our reality. Only identification with the True Self can provide the reality, substance, love and fulfillment we yearn for.

To connect with our True Self, we have to reclaim the shadow self and transform our repressed energies. Integration literally means to join or unite. It is the opposite of separation and necessary if we hope to become whole. We have to take back what we have denied or projected in order to heal it. We have to bring the darkness to light to dispel it.

Consciously deciding to accept and work with our thoughts and feelings is a start but it's not enough. The conscious mind is just a tiny portion of mind. Much bigger and more powerful is what lies below the surface. It is there that the patterns of thoughts and emotions that unconsciously drive our lives reside. That is what we need to bring to the surface.

PROCESS

1. I feel _____ because I think/believe
_____.

EXAMPLE: I feel fearful because I think I will lose my job.

We identify with our thoughts and emotions. Changing them arouses resistance. So next, we must ask…

2. What benefits am I getting from that thought? Why do I want to believe that?

EXAMPLE: I want to believe I will lose my job because _____.

Keep filling in the answer. Sit and wait for more thoughts to arise even after you think you have covered everything.

EXAMPLE: I want to believe I will lose my job because: I don't think I deserve to keep it. I'm not very good at it. I don't really like my job. Part of me wants to be fired. I can collect unemployment.

3. What does this situation remind you of? What pattern are you repeating?

EXAMPLE: I'm repeating a pattern of letting decisions be made for me.

4. What belief does the pattern reinforce?

EXAMPLE: I don't have the courage to make decisions. I'm a victim of other people's decisions.

Feelings are stronger vibrations of energy than thoughts. That is why it is so important to get in touch with them. They are the guiding forces of behavior. The woman in this process may think one thing (I want to keep this job) but the way she really feels (I don't like working here) is a much stronger creative force. Her fear will likely come true. She will be fired and will see herself a victim – again. In truth, she will be getting what she really wants. But by pretending that she doesn't want to lose her job, she can play the innocent victim. She will imagine being fired was done to her rather than by her. She'll get unemployment and her friends will sympathize with her. No way is she about to give up the victim role! We resist giving up roles and behavior that have served a purpose. That's why releasing a major pattern takes repeated effort. Old patterns often need to be unraveled thread by thread.

When people embark on the metaphysical path and discover visualization and affirmation, they tend to use those tools like magic wands. They think they can bypass the time and effort necessary to effect lasting change. They hope to solve problems simply by envisioning and affirming the solution. Imagine claiming and visualizing wealth while anxiously worrying about how you're going to pay the rent. The feeling of fear is far stronger than the dream of wealth and will be the attracting force. That's why trying to attract something we believe we lack will fail. In fact, we can actually end up producing more lack.

THE SUBCONSCIOUS MANIFESTS PROOF OF
OUR BELIEFS, NOT WHAT WE WANT TO
BELIEVE

Marjorie was overweight. Diets hadn't worked; maybe visualization and affirmation would. She plastered pictures of skinny people all over her house, in the car, the drawers of her desk at work. Hundreds of times through the day, she repeated, "I am skinny." Marjorie started seeing skinny people everywhere, everywhere but in her mirror. According to the scale, her weight was rising not falling.

Does this mean visualization and affirmation don't work? They were working perfectly, just not as Marjorie hoped. She pretended she could magically nullify the effect of fattening foods with words and images, but she didn't really believe that. So she continued to out-picture what she did believe – the image of herself as a fat person. And she actually gained more weight because she had unwittingly created a conflict between her conscious and subconscious minds. It's as if beliefs or roles we seek to release rise up and do battle with us. That's why things may get worse before they get better.

Conscious mind: I am skinny.

Subconscious mind: No you're not; you're fat. Here's proof.

REPROGRAMMING TOOLS ACTIVATE OPPOSING PATTERNS

According to the Law of the Vacuum, two opposing things cannot occupy the same place at the same time. We have to release the subconscious patterns producing our present experience before a new pattern can be established. Otherwise, opposing thoughts go up against each other and the strongest ones win.

Think of your mind as a garden. You want to pull out the

weeds so flowers can grow. Negative thoughts and counterproductive energies are weeds that have to be removed before new ones can flourish. But some patterns are deeply rooted and we plant over them instead of removing them. When they sprout up again and produce results, we tend to lose faith in our efforts and reconfirm belief in the old program. If our negative beliefs did not produce effects, we would not know what is hidden in our subconscious garden, what needs to be corrected.

Visualization and affirmation work when they are used in conjunction with releasing conflicting patterns of thought, emotion and behavior. Marjorie's image of herself as a fat person was much older and stronger than her dream of having a skinny body. To effect change, she would have to…

1. undo the belief that she was a victim of her body.
2. forgive anyone or anything she was projecting blame on for being fat.
3. recognize the purpose her fat was serving.

Patterns and problems unravel when we cease to feed them with attention, emotion and belief, but it takes time, consistent effort and faith in the process. The good news is that every thought that is corrected, every piece of past programming that is erased, has far reaching effects. Patterns of thought and emotion are interconnected. Loosen one string and the whole fabric begins to come unravel.

Obsess over a problem and it grows bigger and heavier and more immovable. Put your hand out in front of you and gradually draw it closer to your face. The hand doesn't get bigger but it seems to. Focusing closely on an object, obsessing over it, blocks awareness and vision of everything else.

Unresolved problems can be defenses. In Marjorie's case, being fat was her excuse for not attracting the opposite sex. It served as a defense against her deeper fear of not being lovable enough to attract a partner.

Problem is a concept we place upon people and situations that are not the way we want them to be. Labeling something a problem is like putting it in a kiln that bakes and solidifies the energy around it. Worry turns up the heat and the problem grows bigger, harder, more immobile. Our minds think we want what we focus on, talk about and think about the most.

Another powerful law of energy is the Law of Praise. Praise injects energy directly into the object of attention. Unfortunately, people often praise pain and problems more than the good in their lives. Health is rarely discussed as passionately as illness.

PRAISE IS LIKE FERTILIZER:
IT MAKES THINGS GROW.

By merely ceasing to judge an issue a problem and worrying about it, we loosen the energy supporting it. As that energy moves, vision expands, we can see possible resolutions. By changing focus of attention, we change what we see!

We cannot solve our problems with the same thinking we used when we created them. Albert Einstein

CONNECTION KEY 12: Look at your negative beliefs. Question their validity. What purpose do they serve?

CHAPTER 13

SELF AWARENESS

Rather than being your thoughts and emotion,
Be the awareness behind them.
Eckhart Tolle

Most of the time, people function on automatic pilot...

> Brains recycle the same thoughts, feelings and
> behavior over and over.

> Thinking isn't thinking at all but automatic
> association.

> We see ourselves, other people and the world
> through a web of past experiences, judgments,
> expectations, fears, desires.

> We superimpose our perceptions and moods upon
> the present.

Much of our attention is on the past and the future. Rarely
do we directly experience the here and now – and that is the
only place we can know our True Self. To see the present
without filters, we need to rise above the grooved,
automatic programming of the brain. The part of mind that
can do that is known as the Witness.

We go into the Witness State simply by stepping back and

watching ourselves, being aware of our thoughts, emotions and physical feelings. Obviously, the Witness must be outside that which it is witnessing. It observes what is happening from a detached, neutral viewpoint, much as you might watch the fingers on your hand tapping a table top. You are aware of what they're doing, aware that they are only part of you and cannot function without your consent and energy; you are the power moving those fingers. So it is with our thoughts, feelings and behavior. They are aspects of consciousness that cannot run without our permission and energy.

We are more than thoughts, emotions and actions since we can virtually step outside and observe them. Mastery over them is achieved through observation. From the Witness state, we can exert the power of choice. We can fall back into an old pattern or choose a new direction.

PROCESS

Watch the images that arise during the following process as if you are watching a movie. Be aware of what your character is doing, thinking and feeling while remaining detached from it all.

1. Find a quiet place where you will not be interrupted. Sit comfortably with your back straight and without crossing your arms and legs.

2. Close your eyes and relax. Take 5 deep inhales through the nose and fully exhale through your mouth.

3. Notice your body and anything that is going on physically. Adjust your position to feel more comfortable.

4. Notice your emotions. What are you feeling right now? Are you peaceful or anxious?

5. Notice the thoughts floating across your mind. Some will try to grab your attention. Let them go. Don't focus on any thought but be aware of its nature. Positive or negative?

6. Try to let all thoughts fall away and be aware of the silence and stillness.

7. When you are ready, take a deep breath and open your eyes.

8. What did you observe about yourself and the nature of your thoughts? Were you able to stop thinking entirely? How did that feel?

In the Witness State, we are aware, non-judgmental, unemotional. By simply watching our minds, meaningless chatter falls away and choices present themselves. The instant we respond to a thought or feeling, we are drawn into it and fall out of the Witness State. That's okay. Don't berate yourself. Just be aware of what you are doing.

To further develop the ability to Witness yourself...

1. Practice observing yourself in different situations. Listen to your words, watch what you do. Be aware of your body language. Note emotional swings. What triggered them?

2. Write an account of your day in the third person. Describe your behavior and experiences as if you were writing about someone else. Consider a problem or negative reaction. Describe it without emotion. Note the automatic, habitual patterns and judgments that came up during the day.

3. Focus on an object and observe everything about it. Imagine you are going to have to draw or recreate the object in some way. You must note every detail before it is removed from view.

4. Observe people. Sit in a public place where you can people watch. Pay attention to your perceptions and automatic judgments. Let them pass and then try to observe people without judgment. Notice how they walk, their body language, clothes, facial expression.

5. Stop frequently through the day and note your thoughts and emotions. Are they positive, clear and purposeful or filled with irrelevant chatter, criticism and self-defeating messages? What effect are they having on you physically?

Normally, we look at the present through the lens of the past. The only way we can truly experience anything or anyone is to come to it open, allowing it to teach us what it is rather than assuming our judgments and labels provide knowledge. The Witness exists in the present moment. It is outside time as well as outside thoughts, emotions and actions. It doesn't judge or even try to understand although understanding often spontaneously occurs.

AWARENESS PUTS US IN THE PRESENT MOMENT.

CONNECTION KEY 13: If you find it difficult to quiet your mind, try chanting. OM is considered a powerful and sacred sound. Take a deep breath and vocalize the syllable slowly. Repeat for five minutes or longer.

CHAPTER 14

FORGIVENESS

We must develop and maintain the capacity to forgive. He who is devoid of the power to forgive is devoid of the power to love. Darkness cannot drive out darkness; only light can do that. Hate cannot drive out hate; only love can do that.
Martin Luther King, Jr.

Unlike conventional forgiveness that is directed outward, true forgiveness is directed inward. It is ourselves we need to forgive because we are harboring the thoughts and feelings that hurt us. Other people may do hurtful, harmful things to us but as Viktor E. Frankl explains in "Man's Search for Meaning, "…man is ultimately self-determining. What he becomes – within the limits of endowment and environment – he has made out of himself. In the concentration camps, for example, in this living laboratory and on this testing ground, we watched and witnessed some of our comrades behave like swine while others behaved like saints. *Man has both potentialities within himself; which one is actualized depends on decisions but not on conditions.*"

We make the world in our own image. We project our thoughts and beliefs, feelings and fears upon it, and see them reflected back to us. If we don't like what we see, we must change what we're projecting. That is accomplished by forgiveness. Forgiveness is life changing because it withdraws projections thus changing the lens through which we view the world and other people.

Barry was sure he could never forgive his ex-wife. She had cheated on him and the subsequent divorce cost him dearly, not just financially. His ex-wife won custody of the children and poisoned their minds against their father. Barry described his feelings for her as pure hatred. It didn't take long to convince him that the hate was poisoning him not his ex-wife. Barry had to do the Release Process that follows a number of times before his hatred began to dissolve. However, the result was not what he hoped for. Without the cloak of hatred he had worn for so long, Barry felt weak and defenseless. Now we were getting close to the real issue that needed to be healed – Barry's belief that he was weak and defenseless, a victim. That is what he really hated, that part of himself. He projected that hatred onto his ex-wife but she was not the cause of it.

Barry's pain came from his belief system. That is what needed to be forgiven – let go, undone, released. To do so, Barry first had to recognize that he wanted to see his ex-wife the way he did. It was a defense against his feelings of weakness and self-hate; it gave him the illusion of innocence. Was this false sense of innocence worth peace of mind and a relationship with his children? Of course not. In his head, Barry made the right choice but emotionally, he had a hard time letting go of anger and blame. He felt like a little voice inside him kept whispering, "Are you sure you want to see her differently? It was so comfortable blaming everything on her. What's the point of this if she isn't going to change?"

We laid out a step by step forgiveness process for Barry.

First, he was to change his focus of attention when he thought of his ex-wife. As a negative thought about her crossed his mind, he was to switch to a positive thought about her. Everyone has good qualities and certainly she had had enough to make him fall in love with her.

Next, he made a consistent effort to speak to and about his wife in a different way. Gradually, he saw progress; the ice between them began to thaw. The real turning point came from doing the process of imagining her in a chair opposite him. He told her how he felt about her, then switched chairs and played her role. Looking at himself through her eyes helped him see how he had hurt and disappointed her over the years. He felt a rush of compassion that wiped out lingering antipathy. Barry's relationship with his ex-wife changed dramatically after that, and today they have a warm friendship and are mutually supportive parents to their children.

As Barry was working on changing his relationship with his ex-wife, he was also working on forgiving his victim consciousness. By changing his self-perception and taking responsibility for his experiences, Barry stopped responding to events as a victim. That doesn't mean he wouldn't meet people who would try to take advantage of him, but he would be more aware and wouldn't blame them if he allowed himself to be taken in. This is an important point...

WE ARE NOT RESPONSIBLE FOR EVERYTHING THAT HAPPENS BUT WE ARE RESPONSIBLE FOR HOW WE EXPERIENCE IT, WHAT IT DOES TO US.

To view things positively does not mean that we like what we see but we do not condemn it. We seek the lesson. We learn from it. People may be unkind and even perpetrate criminal acts against us, but they are not in control of our thoughts and emotions. They cannot take our peace of mind. We have to give that away.

True forgiveness means letting go of the pain as well as the blame. To do that, we must discover the thoughts behind our emotions and change them. They are the real source of the pain. Remember Bill and JoAnn? She embarrassed him in front of another couple. Embarrassment like anger is a secondary emotion. It is covering a sense of inadequacy, foolishness, inferiority. These are the thoughts and feelings Bill needed to face and forgive. If we are truly comfortable with ourselves, we will not be affected by what other people say about us. Until we reach that point of clarity, just looking at disturbing thoughts and emotions with honesty releases pent up energy and allows healing to begin.

When we reject or condemn another, we are actually rejecting a part of ourselves. This increases self separation and separation from others. Believing that we are individual and separate from the rest of life is the real source of suffering, the cause of fear, guilt, defensiveness and neediness.

Grievances always involve separation and projection. We blame people...

> 1) for what they did. Some acts are cruel and immoral, and clearly warrant correction. However, when we vehemently judge and attack people for their actions, it is a signal that we are projecting on them. When we want to murder the murderers, we are condemning them for the same thing we are

doing in our minds.

2) for how their action affects us. We are not responsible for another's actions, but we are responsible for our reaction.

PROCESS

1. Who do you resent in your life? (Work with one person at a time)

EXAMPLE: My stockbroker

This person *represents* a part of yourself you need to forgive.

2. Why do you resent this person? What has s/he done?

EXAMPLE: Gave me bad advice and made me lose money.

3. What part of yourself are you projecting? Have you done the same thing – in content if not form? In this particular case, appropriate questions would be: Have you given bad advice? Has someone suffered because of your guidance?

EXAMPLE: I gave my son the wrong advice and he took a job he doesn't enjoy.

This is something the subject feels guilty about. He needs to forgive himself for this or he will keep creating situations where people mislead him so he can project his guilt on them.

4. What thoughts and feelings are being resonated?

EXAMPLE: In the situation with the stockbroker, the subject would feel angry, stupid for trusting him. In regard to his son, the subject feels guilty.

These are feelings the subject wants to disown but needs to accept and release.

5. Take responsibility.

EXAMPLE: I am responsible for my thoughts and feelings. I'm really angry at myself for relying on the stockbroker too much and mad at myself for giving my son the wrong advice.

6. How does that make you feel?

EXAMPLE: Stupid. Guilty.

Facing the truth about yourself can arouse guilt and make you direct anger inward. That is the same mistake as projecting blame outward! Don't fall into the trap of redirecting anger and guilt instead of healing it. Confronting the truth about yourself will make you stronger.

7. Forgive yourself. Nurture feelings of self-acceptance and compassion. Focus on lessons learned.

EXAMPLE: As this father lets go of self-condemnation, his vision will expand. As he ceases to blame the stockbroker and takes responsibility, he may see that his son has depended on him too much.

8. Replacement. This is the time to focus on how you can use this issue/situation to grow, qualities

you want to embrace and possible changes you wish to make going forward.

EXAMPLE: The father is likely to do more research before investing. He may decide to encourage more self-reliance in his son.

Just as the stockbroker and father gave the wrong advice, the person who hurt you may have done stupid, cruel or criminal things. But they are not responsible for the emotional pain you *continue* to experience. Grievances, no matter how seemingly justified, nourish and sustain pain. Forgiveness sets us free; we are the ones who reap its benefits. Forgiveness releases the past and liberates the future. It undoes blocks in our minds and hearts that stifle the full, free flow of love.

FORGIVENESS

They speak of reincarnation
And I wonder, if it's so,
Perhaps our paths have crossed before
Not so very long ago.

And did I do unto your soul
What you now do to me?
And are we only working out
A debt to set us free?

Or perhaps you haven't been here
As often yet as I;
Nor had the time to overcome
The faults that I decry.

And even in this present life
I was not at your side
To feel the things that rent your heart
And know what made you cry.

What myriad of thoughts and feelings
Knit the fabric of your being?
Am I to judge you right or wrong
On the little that I'm seeing?

There is much of life ahead,
And I have much to do.
If I would have forgiveness
I must grant it first to you.

For should I hold my grudges,
And you hold yours for me,
We bind our souls with iron links
Through all eternity.

By Geri O'Neill (originally printed in MAKE THE BEST
OF THE REST OF YOUR LIFE)

CONNECTION KEY 14: What negative thoughts about yourself do you need to forgive, release and let go?

CHAPTER 15

GRATITUDE

If the only prayer you ever say is Thank you, that is enough.
Meister Eckhart

In preceding chapters, 'healing feelings' referred to healing painful emotions. Those words can also suggest feelings that heal. In that regard, one of the greatest healing feelings is gratitude. It is a powerful energy, much stronger than simply being thankful or appreciative. If I drop a dollar and a stranger picks it up and hands it to me, I'm thankful; I appreciate the courtesy. But if I drop my credit card and he follows me a block to give it back, I am more than appreciative. I'm thrilled. I'm enriched not only by the return of the card but my brief encounter with this stranger. I am moved by his honesty and decency. My gratitude gives rise to a great attitude.

That's how I like to think of gratitude = great attitude. G.K. Chesterton said, "I would maintain that thanks are the highest form of thought; and that gratitude is happiness doubled by wonder." Wonder and joy are the radiant threads of gratitude. They can transform a life. Do you have moments of wonder in your day? Unfortunately, we usually become complacent about the wonders that abound and all our blessings. After a while, we take health, relationships and possessions for granted. This is a sad fact of human nature. One researcher explained, "When any event occurs to us, we make it ordinary. And through it becoming ordinary, we lose our pleasure." Grateful people don't have that problem. Nor do children. They never tire of a favorite story or teddy bear. They laugh louder every time the same joke is repeated. They find mundane things fascinating. Their lives are filled with wonder.

Animals are wondrous creatures and can teach us about wonder. Dogs greet their loved ones with unbounded joy *every* time they see them. They easily make friends with strangers. They love to play and they explore the world with wonder. No matter how many times the same path has been tread, every walk is eagerly approached as if there are treasures out there. And there are. For all of us.

Gratitude is a great attitude but like everything else, it dies of neglect. Oh, we may be thankful for what we have, but to experience the power of gratitude, we have to reflect on our blessings long enough to resonate a deep, inner sense of joy and enthusiasm that enriches emotions and brightens outlook. To start your day in a wondrous way, spend a few moments each morning focusing all your attention on your blessings. During the day contemplate the wonders of the world we inhabit – electricity, cars, computers, television, phones and everything in nature! Let the glorious feelings of gratitude and wonder bubble up inside you.

As explained in Chapter 11, present state of mind affects memories, so gratitude can change our picture of the past. We can alter experience by looking at it with gratitude. In the book *Jonathon Livingston Seagull*, we find these words: "every problem has a gift for you in its hands. You have the problem because you need the gift." Singer Tom Jones had a serious problem when he was 12 years old. He developed tuberculosis. He could not go to work in the dark mines of his native Wales as was expected. It seemed he had no future, but he went on to become a world famous celebrity. How often disappointments in our lives turn out to be for the best, and setbacks steer us in new and better directions. Feeling grateful for everything lets the good come forth.

I have a chapter on gratitude in my book *Make The Best Of The Rest Of Your Life* that bears repeating here: "Gratitude is like an electrical light switch. It turns on light and erases darkness. With gratitude we can switch perception from problem to opportunity, from resistance to acceptance, from ending to beginning, from sickness to healing, from anger to forgiveness. Easier said than done? Not really. Find just one thing to feel truly grateful for in the midst of any situation and it is so powerful that it will overcome other emotions. Once you turn on gratitude, it keeps flowing and growing."

Gratitude is like a tender hand that goes out and blesses everything it touches. If you doubt the effect of gratitude, notice what happens when it isn't offered. We're crushed when our acts of courtesy aren't acknowledged with a simple thank you. If our efforts or gifts aren't gratefully recognized, we lose heart. On the other hand, gratitude is a magic potion that lifts spirits, heals discord, raises self-esteem. Practice gratitude every day, in every situation, and your life will be filled with wonder, joy and love.

This is a wonderful day. I've never seen this one before.
Maya Angelou

CONNECTION KEY 15: Write down 3 things a day you are grateful for. Try not to repeat anything from day to day. At the end of a month, enjoy reading your list.

CHAPTER 16

RELEASE

You empower what you fight.
You withdraw power from what you release.
Alan Cohen

Emotions are neither right or wrong, nor good or bad. They are simply energy waves seeking expression and release. There are appropriate ways to express them, ways that heal body and mind. There are also negative ways to release energy that increase pain in the long run. Emotional outbursts, for instance, let off steam but have a negative backlash and add more fuel to the fire within.

Releasing pent up feelings in a positive way opens the energy field and allows trapped, distorted energy to move out. When we release painful feelings and negative mental patterns, perception automatically changes. We see and experience life differently; we feel more alive.

It doesn't matter where self-defeating thoughts came from. The problem is holding onto them. If the goal is to continue blaming someone for your pain, you will never get over it. If, however, you are ready to release negative emotions, the Release Process will be of great benefit. Feeling feelings allows them to move and vibrate out.

You will be asked to focus on a strong emotion. Consider

your emotional triggers; they stir repressed energy that needs to be discharged. Judgments, feelings and automatic reactions in the course of a day are signals that tell us what we need to look at, forgive and release. There may be a particular person or situation presently disturbing you. Facial expression, physical sensations and music can be used to stimulate emotion. Some music stirs deep feelings of sadness. You may choose to work with something that came up while doing a process in this book. There are additional processes at the end of this chapter sure to resonate emotions.

No matter what you focus on, the important thing is to stay with whatever feelings arise. We automatically resist pain but that is what locks it inside. Now we want to do the opposite, invite the pain to come forth. Underneath the pain, misperceptions, fear and guilt, the True Self resides.

Some of the things you may experience during release:

> Breathing changes
> Sighs, moans or crying
> Physical twitches
> Muscle spasms
> Tingling/vibration
> Coughing or runny nose
> Chills, Perspiration

You may wish to talk, cry, sigh, scream during the process. It's energy moving; let it happen. After a little while, you will feel a deep shift and sense of relief. Following the release, you may feel lighter and energized or you could feel tired, the relaxing fatigue that follows a good work out. Listen to your body. Allow a period of adjustment.

Due to unfamiliarity, you may resist the process in the

beginning and nothing seems to happen. Even then, there will be subtle changes in your energy field. As you learn to trust the process and surrender to it, there will be more obvious effects. After you do the Release Process a few times, you will remember the procedure. At first, you might want to record the directions and play them back. If you have a partner or friend who wishes to do the process as well, you can guide each other through it. As you become familiar with the process, modify and design what works best for you.

NOTE: It is best to do the process when you don't have anything scheduled afterward.

PREPARATION: Go to the bathroom before beginning. Wear loose, comfortable clothing. Remove shoes, jewelry, glasses. Have Kleenex handy. Lie comfortably on the bed or floor in a quiet room where you will not be disturbed. Do not cross arms or legs.

Say, "It is safe for me to look at my negative thoughts and painful feelings. It is only my own mind I am looking at. I am in control. I am safe."

BREATHING: Close your eyes and do 5 connected breaths. Inhale deeply through the nose immediately followed by a full exhale through the mouth and repeat. Fall into a comfortable rhythm of steady, deep breathing.

RELAXATION: Imagine the breath moving through your body as you tell each area to relax and open. Attain a state wherein you are fully relaxed but alert. Maintain a comfortable rhythm of steady, deep breathing.

FOCUS: From the Witness State, observe your physical reaction as you focus on an upsetting situation, something that arouses strong emotions in you – fear, sorrow, guilt, hate, anxiety, anger, defensiveness etc. Allow the feelings to rise. Do not analyze or judge them.

EXPLORE: You are more than your thoughts and emotions. Remain in the Witness State as you observe your physical and emotional reaction. Imagine you're describing in detail what is going on within you to someone who can't see what's happening. You may not literally see shapes and colors but you can sense or imagine what the energy looks like.

Where is the feeling located in the body?
What does it feel like?
What does it look like?
What color is it?
What image would you use to describe it?

Keep breathing and watch as emotions become fuller, more powerful. They might move around in your body, change shape and color.

ENTRY: The feeling grows stronger and you are having difficulty staying detached. It is getting bigger, trying to pull you in. Let go. Allow yourself to fall into the feeling. Become one with it, one with the guilt or anger or sadness or fear. Immerse yourself in the feeling. No resistance. No thoughts. You are the feeling. Surrender completely to it. Let it absorb you.

BREATHE: Keep breathing as you allow the feeling to take over. Don't try to control the energy. Let it move. There may be tears and physical reactions. Let them occur. Stay with what's happening.

RELEASE: Say, "I am willing to feel this feeling and I am willing to let it go." Breathe it out. Sound it out. Cry it out. Sigh it out. Ride the feeling out on the breath. See it flowing out of your energy field like a wave.

Keep scanning your body. Notice any areas that are trying block the energy flow. Focus on the tightness/resistance. As you inhale, increase the tension in that area. Hold it, then relax completely as you fully exhale and say, "Relax and release." Keep repeating those words as you breathe into and through that spot. Visualize it opening.

SHIFT: When repressed energy is released, there is a shift. The body relaxes. Breathing and facial expression change. There may be different physical sensations. Remain in this space for a while and let the body adjust.

TRANSITION: You have been carrying that energy for a long time. Now you may feel a void, an open space in your energy field. You could feel vulnerable, empty or sad. Relax into that space without trying to change it.

REPLACEMENT: Your energy field is wide open now and pure energy can flow to you and through you. Breathe deeply as you picture light and love and peace moving freely and fully through you. See your body, mind and heart bathed in those energies. (Replacement will be described more fully in the next chapter).

AFTER RELEASE: Allow yourself time to rest in a relaxed, peaceful state. You may feel like you're floating. You could fall asleep.

IMMEDIATE EFFECTS can include increased sensitivity, symptoms of sickness like tearing, a runny nose, sneezing. You could feel energized or extremely tired. Relax and take it easy allowing time for your energy field to reconfigure.

SIGNS OF HEALING: Increased vitality. Sharper senses. Feeling more open, accepting and loving.

Just as it took many years to create the false self, it takes time to remove the layers that stand between us and our True Self. The following processes can help you get in touch with repressed energy.

PROBING THE HIDDEN SELF

THE INNER CHILD

Would you let an angry, hurt, irrational child make your life decisions? No, of course not. But wait, that's exactly what we do. Many of the beliefs we have about ourselves and life were formed by a child. To grow up, we have to undo the limiting patterns that evolved out of childhood experience. Following are questions designed to trigger such patterns. When a question resonates strong feelings and memories, stop and use the forgiveness or Release Process.

AS A CHILD...

1. What was the most humiliating/embarrassing thing that happened to you?

2. What secrets did you keep out of shame, guilt or fear?

3. What were you punished for, made to feel guilty about?

4. What were you unjustly accused of?

5. What conclusions did you form about money?

People? Food? Sex?

6. What frightened you most?

7. What part of yourself were you ashamed of?

8. What were you forced to do against your will?

9. What is the saddest memory you have of your childhood?

10. Who was unkind to you? What hurt you the most?

11. What did you dislike about your mother? Father? Siblings?

12. What do you most wish you could change about your childhood?

THE STAGES OF LIFE

Apply similar questions to the different stages of your life...

TEENAGER: What are the strongest memories of your teenage years? What was most important to you then? Did you achieve your goals? What were your biggest disappointments? Fears? What were you ashamed of? What did you resent? What made you angry?

ADULT: What thoughts, feelings or actions are you ashamed of? Did you cheat, lie, steal to get where you are? Who did you disappoint? Hurt? If you were famous, what would you most fear the media finding out about you? Who would you not want the press to interview about you?

SENIOR: What have you failed at? What are your fears, disappointments, regrets? What one thing do you most wish you could change about your past? About yourself?

SELF-LOVE

At first, the following process may make you very uncomfortable. Accept the feelings that come up and use the Release Process to experience and express the energy.

1. Sit comfortably facing a full length mirror.

2. Say to your image, "I love you." Slowly, sincerely, keep repeating those words.

3. Voice the thoughts and feelings that arise in response to that statement. After verbalizing each thought, and feeling the resistance, unworthiness, denial or embarrassment, breathe the energy out. Say, "I am willing to feel these feelings and I am willing to let them go."

4. Continue the process until you can say, "I love you," without resonating any resistance.

The goal is to be able to remain clear and feel love for yourself when you say the words. As understanding and compassion for self grows, we become more understanding and accepting of others.

ENERGY SHIFTERS

Healing feelings and releasing repressed energy clears inner channels for the full, pure expression of the True Self. But sometimes "the world is too much with us" as William Wordsworth said. When that happens and we feel ourselves losing awareness, being pulled down or drawn back to old, automatic responses, we need to stop and shift our energy. Following are quick, easy energy shifters.

Move – Exercise, stretch, walk, dance

Get rid of stuff – Clean out your closets, desk, car

Forget yourself – do something for someone else

Meditate, chant

Listen to soothing music and drink a cup of herbal tea

Pamper yourself. Take a bath, get a massage

Verbalize thoughts and feelings aloud

Write about your thoughts and feelings

Draw a picture of your feelings

Release the need to understand

Make a stranger smile

Focus on the feeling of gratitude

Write a note of appreciation to someone

Buy someone a small present (under 5 or 10 dollars)

Buy yourself a small present (under 5 or 10 dollars)

Play a game

Smile, smile, smile. Smiling sends a message to your brain and body that everything is okay. It reduces stress hormones and releases feel good hormones.

Laugh, laugh, laugh. Laughter has countless physical and psychological benefits. It releases tension, broadens perspective and transcends negativity.

If you are depressed, you are living in the past.
If you are anxious, you are living in the future.
If you are at peace, you are living in the present.
Lao Tzu

CONNECTION KEY 16: The clearer you become, the faster you will be able to release emotional upsets as they occur. When disturbed, stop what you're doing and feel the feeling. Say to yourself, "I am willing to feel this and willing to let it go." Breathe it out.

CHAPTER 17

REPLACEMENT

When we quit thinking primarily about ourselves and our own self-preservation, we undergo a truly heroic transformation of consciousness.
Joseph Campbell

When we embark on a metaphysical or spiritual path, it is usually with the goal of making the self we think we are better, more capable of getting what it wants. We use reprogramming tools and practices to get things we think will make us happy or to inspire behavior and actions we hope will win fame and fortune. All this merely creates another false self. A nice one, very appealing no doubt, but still false. And it will stand as a barrier against the True Self just as rigidly as the other one did. Perhaps more so since we are likely to value it more. In time, however, it too will fail to provide what we hoped for. We will find that we're still not *really* happy, peaceful and fulfilled. That's when the search for the True Self begins. That's when we are required to go beyond the self we think we are.

As we drop identification with the false self, we can begin to consciously identify with the True Self. Now is the time to use visualization and affirmation, but not as we have in the past. Our goal now is to transcend the personal self not change it. When we are ready to surrender to our True Self, we can use these tools to attune to its essence.

PROCESS: Close your eyes, breathe deeply and relax. Focus full attention on qualities associated with the True Self – peace, light, love, joy. Visualize the essence of these pure energies flowing through your being. Claim it with words. Attune to it energy and then stop. Let it flow. Breathe your mind, heart and energy field open. You are calling forth those qualities, inviting them to penetrate your being.

The pure energy of the True Self automatically flows to us and through us if our mental and emotional channels are clear. Albert Schweitzer wrote about the experience in these words: *Your life is something opaque not transparent, as long as you look at it in an ordinary human way. But if you hold it up against the light of God's goodness, it shines and turns transparent, radiant, and bright. And then you ask yourself in amazement: Is this really my own life I see before me?*

It can be both startling and dismaying to face the fact that the self we have identified with is just a role we're playing in a story we're caught up in. As we release the various lies and layers of the false self and begin to detach from it, it is common to experience a sense of emptiness, a void within. The word avoid means to evade, stay away from. Most people avoid the void at any cost. Who will we be without our assortment of costumes and masks? The tendency is to rush to fill the void, to quickly re-clothe ourselves in the false identity.

Remember the Law of the Vacuum? Nature abhors an empty space. Surely you've cleaned out a junk drawer in your house only to have it fill to overflowing again in days.

So it is with our minds. We tend to fall back into old personas and regenerate past patterns unless there is something new to take its place. There is, but to experience it, we have to allow ourselves to experience the silence, the void.

PROCESS

Set aside 30 minutes and don't *do* anything. Don't read, talk, watch television or listen to music. A sense of anxiety will arise almost immediately, a desire to do something. Feel the anxiety. Don't resist. Breathe through it.

After the initial resistance, the body and mind start to settle down. Thoughts drift away. At this point, a feeling of emptiness surfaces. Allow yourself to sink into it.

Feelings of guilt or fear or sadness arise as we come face to face with the empty spaces in ourselves and our lives. We equate nothingness with death, but the void is in fact the matrix of creativity. Among the many gifts to be found in allowing ourselves to merge with the void are greater awareness, insight, sensitivity, pure emotion and clear perception. Out of the void new ideas and possibilities arise. We need to sink into and experience the void, and stay with it. It is the fertile soil of the soul. From it rises the phoenix, the new life.

The following meditations can also help in establishing and maintaining connection to the True Self.

MEDITATIONS: Following are three separate meditations. Always start with deep, steady breathing and relaxing the body. Let thoughts drift away. Stay open, aware and maintain focus.

> 1. Light is the essence of all that is. It is pure energy. Identification with light purifies the body and mind. See yourself surrounded by light. Feel it moving into and through your body. Your organs, bones, blood, cells are all illuminated with light. It is so bright, so powerful that it radiates from you.

> 2. Fear constricts the energy field. Love opens it. On the inhale, feel the heart area in the middle of your chest open. Say, "I am open and receptive to love." On the exhale, feel your mind and body absorbing that love.

> 3. Listen. Focus every thought, feeling and cell of your body on listening. Listen intently. Do not let tiny sounds distract you. Listen to what is behind them. Listen deeper until you are immersed in utter silence.

Deal with judgments, negative thoughts and feelings as they arise. Release them and replace them with the love and light of your True Self. Listen and let its guidance lead you.

The Self is not a goal to be attained, it is merely the awareness that prevails when all the limiting ideas about the not-Self have been discarded. Ramana Marharshi

CONNECTION KEY 17: Wherever you are, whatever you're doing, take a deep breath, envision and feel light, love and joy moving to you and through you.

CHAPTER 18

LOVE

All my life, my heart has yearned for a thing I cannot name.
Andre Breton

If we were to describe the True Self in one word, that word would be Love. But do we know what love is? The concept of love held by most people differs markedly from the pure Love that is the essence of the True Self. We grow up thinking the love we yearn for is hidden in other people but Love comes from within and is not dependent on anything external. We expect love to be focused exclusively on us and ours but Love is not confined to specifics; it is all encompassing. We live in fear of love dying, our loved ones leaving us. Love does not waver; it is infinite and constant. The love we have grown up idolizing and seeking does not make us whole. It does the opposite. The more we depend on externals for love, approval and value, the needier we feel.

Anxiety is love's greatest killer, because it is like the strangle hold of the drowning. Anais Nin

Love turns to hate when lovers fail to fulfill us. As the illusion of love crumbles, we see our love idols as the same imperfect beings we are. The mirror image is so distasteful that we are quick to reject that person and go in search of another. All external searches for love and fulfillment will fail. No matter how much we may be appreciated or what we achieve or gain, it will never be enough. It will be a sedative but sedatives wear off leaving an even more acute sense of emptiness within.

> *There is only one kind of love, but there are a thousand imitations.*
> Francois de La Rochefoucauld

The True Self is the source of Love. The greater the disconnection from it, the greater the yearning for Love. This yearning is what will eventually set us on the path to reunite with our True Self. Until such time, our search is misdirected – we look outside for what can only be found inside. We are driven to find purpose in work, value in things, approval in relationships. We think money will give us the possessions and status and emotions we crave. In fact, these things act as defenses against confronting our dark side and thus erect more barriers against the True Self and real Love.

	TRUE LOVE	**FALSE LOVE**
SOURCE	Internal	External
FOCUS	Content	Form
GOAL	Inclusion	Exclusion
NATURE	Unconditional	Conditional
	Liberating	Binding
EFFECTS	Fulfillment	Neediness
	Peace	Excitement
	Trust	Anxiety
	Wholeness	Dependency

PROCESS

1. What do you most hope to gain from worldly experience or relationships?

EXAMPLE: Approval, recognition

2. You have denied that to yourself or you would not be looking outside for it.

As long as we look outside for love and fulfillment, there is no hope of lasting happiness much less awakening. Why then do we keep spinning around on this merry go round? Ironically, we fear the thing we crave. What if merging with our True Self/Love destroys us as human beings? What if we are catapulted out of this world and away from all we cherish here? What if we are not worthy of Love and are rejected by it? These fears are at the root of the great existential conflict: the desire to be one with the True Self and separate at the same time. We long for it, search for it, strive for it, and erect barricades against it.

This conflict undermines our worldly love relationships and desire for happiness. We choose the 'wrong' people to fall in love with: people we can't be with for one reason or another, or someone who doesn't reciprocate our interest. We pick petty arguments with partners in order to put some emotional if not physical distance between us. Watch yourself getting close to love, happiness and fulfillment, then sabotaging it. We fear the very thing we yearn for because we don't know what the True Self actually is, and we naturally fear the unknown.

While the True Self/Love must be experienced to be known, there are things we know about it. Virtually every school of spiritual thought would agree that the True Self is pure Love, light, peace and joy. It is the opposite of fear and guilt and so, dissolves them. It is the opposite of darkness and so, erases it. Why would we not want to experience this, to live like this? In the end, it is our attachment to the false self that presents the biggest obstacle to union. We identify with our patterns and problems. Our dramas and traumas are the food the false self feeds on. Sooner or later, we will tire of it all and realize that love is not about physical union, but the union of spirits; not about being loved but loving. Fulfillment does not come from getting but giving, not from gratification but compassion. Peace comes not from winning but forgiving. When that realization dawns, we will forge ahead and embrace our True Self.

Anwar Sadat was president of Egypt from 1970 until October 1981 when he was assassinated by fundamentalists. He won the Nobel Peace Prize for his efforts at establishing peace between Egypt and Israel. His early revolutionary activities to overthrow British rule in his country landed him in jail where he experienced enlightenment. He describes it in these words:

Once released from the narrow confines of the 'self'...a man will have stepped into a new, undiscovered world which is vaster and richer...my narrow self ceased to exist and the only recognizable entity was the totality of existence, which aspired to a higher, transcendental reality.

One of the surest ways to connect with the True Self is by practicing kindness. Kindness warms the coldest hearts, eases the sorrow of the unhappiest soul, gives hope to the downtrodden and renews the broken hearted. Sincere, loving kindness seeks no reward. Many years ago, I was driving my father who was quite ill from upstate New York to south Florida; he had insisted on making the drive with me rather than flying. We encountered all manner of problems along the way. It was a Murphy's Law trip all the way: whatever could go wrong did go wrong. When we reached north Florida, my father finally agreed to take a plane for the rest of his journey.

After seeing him off at the airport, I was driving back to my friend's home in Ponte Vedra Beach to spend the night. As I was crossing the bridge over the Intracoastal waterway, there was a huge whoosh and the car started to shudder & shake. I made it to the shoulder of the road, turned off the ignition, got out & saw that the front tire was flatter than a pancake. My spirits sank flatter than that. For my father's sake, I had stayed strong and positive and handled each hurdle as best I could, but I had reached my limit. I had no resources left.

In that instant, I felt like my soul was laid bare. I watched cars drive by. Some part of me knew I should put my hand out for help; I couldn't even do that. Finally, I turned & walked to the railing. Looking out over the water, I said aloud, "I give up. I've got nothing left." At that moment a pickup truck with Georgia plates pulled up behind me. A long, lean man stepped out and said in a lovely Georgia drawl, "You got a flat tire?" Actually he said, "You got a flat tar?" I nodded. "I be happy to fix that flat tar for you." I started to cry. Can you imagine someone being *happy* to fix a flat tire for you? More miraculous than fixing the tire was the spirit in which he did it – so kind, so generous of heart & hand with no thought of return.

It took nearly an hour to unpack and repack the overloaded trunk and fix the tire. I tried to press some money upon him. He refused. In fact, he was shocked. He said, "I cain't take money from you. You was in distress. Maybe someday I be in distress & somebody stop & help me." I hope the same kindness he showed me was returned to him many times over.

To be the beneficiary of such gentle kindness is a spiritual experience. From the depths of despair, I was lifted up. Another reason that experience was so powerful for me is that I realized I had to give up, surrender so to speak. We have to let go before the True Self can take over.

Two ways to hasten reunion with the true Self: give up control and be truly kind to every person in every situation. That doesn't mean we let people have their way if they are in error. Our response and actions would be appropriate but without condemnation. The clearer we become, the more we will see the light in one another rather than the faults. Where there is error, we will correct without criticizing, guide without controlling and discern without judging.

To live content with small means; to seek elegance rather than luxury, and refinement rather than fashion; to be worthy, not respectable, and wealthy, not rich; to study hard, think quietly, talk gently , act frankly; to listen to stars and birds, to babes and sages, with open heart; to bear all cheerfully, do all bravely, await occasions, hurry never. In a word, to let the spiritual, unbidden and unconscious, grow up through the common. This is to be my symphony. William Henry Channing

Love is the natural state of pure energy. When love is not present, we need to look at what is blocking it. With love, one is naturally compassionate, honest, moral. There is no question or right or wrong. All things inspired by love are right.

Love looks past the façade to the light within.

Love is a force that moves through individual channels but there is no sense of individuality.

Live with kindness and love will follow.

CONNECTION KEY 18: Kindness blesses the giver as well as the receiver. How can you be a little kinder in your thoughts, words and actions – to yourself? To others?

CHAPTER 19

INTO THE UNKNOWN

As you move outside of your comfort zone, what was once the unknown and frightening becomes your new normal.
Robin S. Sharma

Perhaps now you better understand why we are drawn toward our True Self and yet resist the pull. We fear the unknown. That is why unravelling patterns takes time. The kinder and more patient we are with ourselves, the easier the process will be. As we undo patterns thread by thread, we receive glimpses of our True Self. Its incredible power, peace and Love begin to emerge. There are moments of pure joy and compassion, spontaneous acts of kindness. We automatically know the right words to say in a trying situation. We never knew such peace. And then the door slams shut!

Attachment to our false self is strong, and old attitudes and grievances creep back in. At one time, I was teaching classes on personal transformation. One assignment was to clean out the house. The following week, one girl was very excited telling how she had packed up four big boxes of stuff, put it in the garage and called Good Will. Suddenly her voice fell, "But Good Will couldn't come for four days and by then I had put it all back."

These episodes are not setbacks even though they seem that

way. If obstacles don't come up to block our path, how are we to know where healing work is needed? The real setback is feeling guilty when we hit a bump in the road, and berating ourselves. That's what made us self-divide in the first place! Simply looking honestly at resistance, fears, guilt and past programming without judging ourselves shines light into the dark corners of the mind.

Internal blocks manifest as ongoing turmoil, conflict, stress and strain. The full free flow of life is stifled, pressure builds up, leaving us drained, unhappy and fearful. These are the places where we need to let go and grow. Resistance to growth, not growth itself, causes pain.

"Come to the cliff," the Papa Bird said to his babies.

"No, no," they cried.

"Come to the cliff," he said.

"We are afraid," they cried.

"Come to the cliff," he commanded.

They came. He pushed them. They flew.

We will come to the cliff again and again until we are ready to let go and fly.

In his book, The Power of Now, Ekhart Tolle writes: *Always say "yes" to the present moment. Whatever the present moment contains, accept it as if you had chosen it. Always work with it, not against it. Make it your friend and ally, not your enemy. This will miraculously transform your whole life.*

What do you need to meet, accept, say yes to, work with instead of against? Don't overburden yourself. Work with one issue at a time. Amazingly, dismantling one mental block has effects on all of them. Be patient and gentle with yourself. There is no reason to fear the re-appearance of a self-defeating thought or unkind feeling as long as you don't let it take over.

If you use the knowledge you've acquired and the processes in this book, you will be able to demolish your blocks. The goal is to become consciously aware and fully alive in the present. The greatest challenge is finding within ourselves the courage to enter the unknown, to give up personal control and trust the True Self to steer our course.

Look into your own selves and find the spark of truth that God has put in every heart and that only you can kindle to a flame. Socrates

CONNECTION KEY 19: What are you holding onto that needs to be released? Where are you stuck? Where do you need to give up, let go?

CHAPTER 20

REMINDERS

The True Self is not our creation, but God's.
It is the self we are in our depths. It is our capacity
for divinity and transcendence.
Sue Monk Kidd

It is my most sincere hope that the information and processes in this book serve as an aide in your quest to undo the barriers that stand between you and your True Self. I should say our True Self for like waves on the sea, we are all part of the one pure life force that is the True Self. The underlying oneness of all is recognized by quantum physicists, pop stars and gurus alike...

Quantum physics thus reveals a basic oneness
of the universe. Erwin Schrodinger

It's difficult to believe in yourself because the idea of self is
an artificial construction. You are, in fact, part of the
glorious oneness of the universe. Everything beautiful in
the world is within you. Russell Brand

All differences in this world are of degree, and not of kind,
because oneness is the secret of everything.
Swami Vivekananda

So know that all your efforts and every step you take toward Love is a blessing to all. As you heal your feelings, your presence will extend a healing feeling to the world.

Our own self-realization is the greatest service we can render the world. Ramana Maharshi

The following lines are snapshots of the ideas presented in this book. They are in no particular order. Read them as a review or focus on one at a time...

Self-separation is the real cause of suffering.

What we believe about others is a reflection of our deepest beliefs about ourselves.

Energy is malleable clay; belief systems are the sculptor.

Perceptions, feelings and physical issues are keys to locked doors of the past.

Emotions spring from interpretation.

As a house divided against itself cannot stand, so a self divided against itself cannot thrive.

We manifest what we believe, not what we want.

Present experiences are tuning forks that resonate corresponding energy within us.

Anger is a defense against painful emotions.

What goes on in the mind comes out in the body.

Internal blocks manifest as ongoing turmoil, conflict, stress and strain.

The past is just an old movie running in the brain.

We see outside what we repressed inside. The world mirrors our thoughts back to us.

We create circumstances that are both vents for repressed feelings and fuel to reinforce them.

Repressed pain, fears and guilt of the past are projected on the present shaping perception and experience.

We don't experience people. We experience our thoughts and feelings about them.

The brain seeks & finds what it's looking for.

Express gratitude to yourself. The more you appreciate yourself, the sooner that energy will overflow and bless others.

Not accepting responsibility makes us victims. Accepting responsibility empowers us.

Repression causes self-division. To heal is to make whole.

Present state of mind determines the past we remember and how we remember it.

Emotions are stronger than thoughts. They are the guiding forces of behavior.

What you praise with your thoughts and words increases.

Judgments and automatic reactions are signals that tell us what we need to look at, forgive and release.

Subconscious beliefs outweigh conscious thought.

Present state of mind and choices affect past and future.

It is ourselves we need to forgive because we harbor the thoughts and feelings that hurt us.

We are more than thoughts, emotions and actions since we can virtually step outside and observe them.

In rejecting or condemning another, we are actually rejecting and condemning ourselves.

Looking is the light that erases darkness.

Love comes from within; it is not dependent on externals.

Chronic physical tension is the result of locking repressed energy into the musculature of the body.

The world is a movie screen. What we see on it is projected by the programs running in our minds.

Forgiveness is letting go of pain as well as blame.

Gratitude is a quick, effective method for changing perceptions and feelings.

The brain produces and attracts evidence of its beliefs.

Resistance causes pain.

We contract our awareness to such a point that it does not perceive reality, only a tiny, distorted fragment of it.

Visualization, affirmation and positive thinking will backfire unless you remove opposing thought systems.

Awakening is a gradual process. Fear not that you will be swallowed up by a volcano of light and disappear.

If your True Self is at the helm, you will feel peace no matter what is happening.

The True Self and pure Love are one and the same.

Facial expressions produce corresponding emotions. A sincere smile has instant, positive effects.

When we accept and integrate the past, it becomes a source of strength not victimization.

As we deceive ourselves as to who and what we are, so also must we deceive others.

Begin to identify with love, not the body.

While we are not responsible for everything that happens around us, we are responsible for what happens in us.

What is your goal? Set your purpose at the outset.

Is what I'm doing going to help or hinder me on my path?

To withhold love is to deprive yourself of it.

Fulfillment does not come from getting but giving.

The feeling of Love comes from loving not being loved.

We don't have to search for the True Self. It will appear when we remove interferences to it.

We are like waves on the sea, all part of the one pure life force that is the True Self.

God is at home, it's we who have gone out for a walk.
Meister Eckhart

Isn't it time to go home?

ABOUT THE AUTHOR

Geri O'Neill is an author, lecturer and metaphysical teacher. She has been presenting seminars and workshops on spiritual awakening, mind and human nature for over 30 years, and has lectured on cruise ships around the world.

Geri's book *MAKE THE BEST OF THE REST OF YOUR LIFE* is a handbook for living a happy, healthy life. Her novel *HEARTSONG* is a mystical love story.

www.gerioneill.com

Read about Geri and her husband's extensive world travels in her blog:

www.highroads.blogspot.com

41721861R00069

Made in the USA
Lexington, KY
24 May 2015